THE RETURN

An end-time epistle to the Church in America

MATTHEW CASEY

" Return to Me, and I will return to you..."
Malachi 3:7

Foreword By CHARLES CRISMIER

Except where otherwise indicated all Scripture quotations are taken from the New King James Version unless specifically noted otherwise.

Verses marked KJV are taken from the King James Version of the Bible.

Packaged by ACW Press
PO Box 110390
Nashville, TN 37222
www.acwpress.com
The views expressed or implied in this work do not necessarily reflect those of ACW Press. Ultimate design, content, and editorial accuracy of this work is the responsibility of the author(s).

Publisher's Cataloging-in-Publication Data
(Provided by Cassidy Cataloguing Services, Inc.)

Casey, Matthew Jonathan.

    The return : an end-time epistle to the church in America / Matthew Casey. -- Richmond, VA : Elijah Books, c2010.

    p. ; cm.
    ISBN: 978-0-9718428-5-4

    1. Christianity--United States--21st century. 2. Revivals--United States--21st century. 3. Second Advent. 4. Judgment Day.
5. Christianity and politics--United States. 6. Christianity and culture--United States. I. Title.

BR526 .C394 2010
277.3/083--dc22   1004

Printed in the United States of America.

CONTENTS

by Charles Crismier

If God Should Speak...

IF GOD SHOULD SPEAK to the Church in America at this momentous hour of human history, what would He say? Would He deliver commendation, bring conviction or perhaps warn of impending condemnation and judgment? Take a moment and ponder. What would our God of mercy, but also of truth, say? Our viewpoint may well determine our destiny.

AN HISTORIC MOMENT

We are living in an historic and prophetic moment. A New World Order has already been declared. A "new order of the ages" is ushering in a global movement, a global economy, a global currency and a global religion. The tributaries of history and prophecy are merging, surging inexorably towards the Second Coming of Christ.

At this propitious moment of history, America—and particularly the Church in America—sits at a crossroads. It may well be the same crossroads that Israel, God's chosen people, faced in the days of Elijah when, in their spiritually compromised condition he cried out confrontingly, "How long halt ye between two opinions? If the LORD be God, follow Him" *(1 Kings 18:21 KJV)*. Since God promised he would again "send unto you Elijah the prophet before the coming of the great and dreadful day of the LORD" (*Malachi 4:5 KJV*), what will He say to those who then claim the name of Christ? What words of wooing and warning might He bring to those occupying the pulpits and pews of America's churches? Perhaps the Apostle John, in the book of Revelation, gives us insight through Jesus' own evaluation of the Seven Churches of Asia (*Revelation 1–3 KJV*).

RESTORING FIRST LOVE

"I know your works, and your labor, and your patience, and how you cannot bear them which are evil…" noted Jesus of the Church at Ephesus. "Nevertheless, I have somewhat against you, because *you have left your first love.* Remember therefore from whence you are fallen, and repent… or I will remove your candlestick except you repent."

Christ's messages to the remaining churches of Asia, representing both the then-time Church and the end-time Church, revealed the profound ways in which **all but one had left their first love** and were in danger of apostatizing from the faith. The warnings were dire and would determine destiny.

AN OVERCOMING CHURCH

Each of the letters to the seven churches of Asia concludes with the words *"to him that overcometh."* The Christ we profess as "Lord" desires and demands that we be overcomers. The pathway to recovering *FIRST LOVE* is defined by confession, repentance, and obedience. If we make the choice, God by His Spirit, will help us make the needed changes.

AN EPISTLE OF MERCY

You now hold in your hands an epistle of mercy and grace to the American Church, a Church which has long since wandered off the highway of holiness (*Isaiah 35:8 KJV*) and is wandering in the wilderness with the prospect of the eternal "promised land" in jeopardy. We have, in major ways, gone back to Egypt in our hearts. And we are lamentably leading the nations to follow our example. Rather than overcoming, we have been overcome with carnality and the spirit of modern or post-modern culture, drifting dangerously toward destruction, wallowing in deception.

For the past generation both Christian and secular polls have determined that there is no meaningful difference between the values and behavior of professing Christians and the secular culture. Even much of our ways of doing "ministry" have been cloned from the secular market. The Master now bows to the Market, and has become a virtual mascot to lend spiritual credibility to largely secular pursuits in the name of "ministry." It is little wonder that in the last decade more missionaries have been sent by the world's countries **to** America than America has sent to the world.

A DECISION FOR DESTINY

VIEWPOINT ALWAYS DETERMINES DESTINY! Just as a merciful, yet just, God wooed and warned the seven Churches of Asia, so His kindness is wooing and warning the Church in America to **repent and return to her first love.** But we... pastor, people, and para-church leader, must agree with the viewpoint of a loving, yet holy, God. For it is written, "Can two walk together unless they be agreed" *(Amos 3:3 KJV)*?

In this loving, yet truth-saturated epistle, Matthew Casey lends his pen to become "the pen of the Lord" to reach a people who, in pride and prosperity, have in many ways become "poor, blind, and naked" *(Revelation 3:17 KJV)* before the eyes of the Lord. It is a message intensely personal yet profoundly corporate.

As president of Save America Ministries, I was both deeply honored yet seriously humbled by the request of our brother in

Christ, Matthew Casey, to write this foreword, recognizing the simple yet daunting truth that destiny rides in the balance of our individual and corporate response. It is our prayerful hope that your heart will be stirred. It is also our confident expectation that if we truthfully, humbly, and joyfully return to our *FIRST LOVE* that God, by His grace and mercy, will enable us as the Church in America to fulfill our holy purpose of preparing the way of the Lord for the "blessed hope of the church," the Second Coming of our Lord and Savior, Jesus Christ.

Yours in His Service,
Preparing the Way of the Lord
for History's final hour,

CHARLES CRISMIER

A Call to Return

DESPERATE TIMES CALL FOR DESPERATE MEASURES, and this is such a time for the American Church. The world sees that something is desperately wrong in our nation, but knows not how to fix it. This is because the answer cannot be found by worldly means or wisdom. *America's only hope lies in a wholehearted return to the God who made her great, in a genuine revival of Biblical proportions.*

"Revival" is a word often used in the Church today, and perhaps more often misused. So what is "a revival?" A revival, as demonstrated in the history of God's people (both in Scripture and in the Church), is:

- A sovereign move of the Most High God;
- Orchestrated by God, not man;
- "Not worked up, but prayed down" as Leonard Ravenhill once said. We cooperate with God by persistent, prevailing prayer. However, we do not create nor earn a revival;
- *A RETURN* of God's people to Himself through repentance;
- *A RETURN* **of God's power and presence to His Church,** resulting in God's name being glorified, God's people being revitalized in love, faith, and obedience, and in the lost being brought to a relationship with God through Jesus Christ.

Genuine revival will (must) include:

- Conviction of sin, leading to the cleansing of our lives and a heart's desire to please God;
- A rekindling of love for Christ; lukewarmth destroyed, passion restored;
- A burden for souls, leading to salvation. A true revival not only revives the saved, but saves the lost;
- Restored hunger for and experience of the Spirit's power and presence in our lives and churches;
- Societal transformation. Genuine revival of the magnitude to which we refer (and which we so desperately need) must bear the fruit of godly change in the society around us;
- Cleansing the altar of God's Church. This invites the Spirit's fire to fall, and endues God's people with His power once again. Such a Church is impossible for the world to ignore or explain away, for true spiritual power demands a response, whether love or hatred.

A.W. Tozer wrote, "We must know again that awe-inspiring mystery which comes upon men and churches when they are full of the power of God." This is the great need of our day, and the purpose of this book is to be one of many voices humbly and lovingly urging the people of God to return.

It is a return to our FIRST LOVE, to faith-filled fellowship with Christ, to the power of the Spirit, and to our intended place of authority and Godly influence. Such a return is America's only hope.

It is time to seek the Lord.

CHAPTER 1

The Time of Shaking Has Begun

...but now He has promised, saying,
"Yet once more I shake not only the earth,
but also heaven." Now this, "Yet once more,"
indicates the removal of those things that are
being shaken, as of things that are made,
THAT THE THINGS WHICH CANNOT
BE SHAKEN MAY REMAIN.

Hebrews 12:26-27

"THOSE THINGS THAT ARE BEING SHAKEN..." As I read this passage in early 2007, I felt quickened with a spiritual urgency to pray for our nation—and specifically for the Church—to be prepared for an intense season of shaking coming to our country.

At that point our economy seemed relatively stable, and most people were in "business as usual" mode. But the next few months would change all of that: joblessness went through the roof while real estate prices fell through the floor. Stalwart investment firms imploded, the stock market failed, and countless fortunes evaporated in a matter of weeks. Even some of the historic anchors of our economy such as the banking and automotive industries were shaken, and two of America's "Big 3" automakers chose government "bailouts" and wound up on welfare. Economic forecasters started using words like "recession" and even the dreaded "depression" to describe what was taking place. And most tragically of all, reports of suicides and family murders flooded the news, as many who lost their fortunes also lost their hope.

The time of the last great shaking has begun. We see it not only in our nation's economy, but also in her politics, in the worldwide rise of militant Islam, in the intensity and frequency of natural calamities, in the dramatic rise of martyrdom for Christ in the last century, and in the global cry for a New World Order.

Things are heating up, and in spite of all the tests and trials this season brings, the Church *ought* to be rejoicing, because the shaking of this world's kingdoms directly precedes the manifestation of that Kingdom which **cannot** be shaken *(see Hebrews 12:28)*. **Christ's return in power and glory is drawing near.**

So why is the American Church not excited about this shaking? *It is because so much of our lives are tied into this world's system and ways.* We trust in its economy, laugh at its entertainment, download its information and embrace (unknowingly) its values. The thought of our nation coming to a place of turmoil and trouble strikes terror into the average churchgoer. *But it need not be so.*

The Scriptures tell us that if we (God's people) will humble ourselves, pray, and repent, **there is yet hope.** Far from fearing the season ahead, we can actually participate in a great harvest God desires for our nation. If we listen to His Word and be led by His Spirit, Christ will make us instruments of His mercy to the lost around us, encouragers of revival in our local churches, and agents of advancing His Kingdom in this late hour.

Even as America is reaping what she has sown and is experiencing the painful consequences of God's discipline, let us recognize:

1. God only disciplines a nation when He still has plans for it. If the Lord simply ignored America's sins, letting us rush headlong into the moral abyss, it would be a sign of unrelenting doom.

However, *the prayers of the saints are prevailing and God has seen fit to send His rod of correction to our nation once more.* I believe this season of shaking will break strongholds of pride and spiritual indifference, ushering in what could be the most significant revival America has ever seen.

2. Shaking is good for the Church, and the Church desperately needs to be shaken out of her slumber. Decades of material abundance and cultural ease have found us drowsily accepting of deadly compromise on the part of those who would lead the American Church. We have substituted the cleverness of man for the power of God's Spirit, chosen inspirational talks over the anointed teaching of God's Word, abandoned real worship for entertainment, made attendance and budget the primary measures of church health, and have adopted this world's mindset regarding success, worth, and significance.

We have tried to do God's work man's way, forsaking "the fountain of living waters" for "broken cisterns" of our own making *(Jeremiah 2:13).* In the absence of the real power and presence of the Holy One, we have fashioned a "golden calf"—a more palatable, culturally acceptable breed of "Christianity"—with the hope that the world will come join our party. *"Maybe if we're more like them, more of them will get saved!"* we have reasoned. On the contrary, we merely prove our shallow experience of Christ by how readily we prostitute His Church to gain the world's acceptance.

The world desperately needs to see a people decidedly NOT like themselves, a people set apart to serve a different God, pursue a different kingdom, and follow a different definition of success. *We must be different in the things that really matter,* starting with *Who* and *how* we love.

This time of shaking will afford many churchgoers the opportunity to truly trust God for the first time, to yield their wills, surrender control of their lives, and learn what it means to be a disciple. In the years ahead, a purified Church will arise in humility and joy, endued with genuine and undeniable spiritual power as we carry the Good News to a dying, deceived, and hurting world.

Sadly, many other churchgoers will fall away *(see 2 Thessalonians 2:3)*. Those whose hearts are not after the King Himself but merely desirous of the blessings they have been taught to expect from Him will depart from the faith *(1 Timothy 4:1)*. The tragic fruit of our excessive teachings—the easy believism, the cheap grace doctrines, the excessive focus on health and wealth that facilitated a gospel of greed, the dead orthodoxy that substituted mere head knowledge for a personal, dynamic relationship with the Living God and which deified systematic theology—these and many other false teachings like them will bear the bitter fruit of disillusionment in the lives of their adherents, and many will fall away. How many thousands of American churchgoing souls will prove to have no oil in their lamps? How many will hear the most sobering words in all of Scripture: "Depart from Me; I never knew you?"

Yes, the hour is late, but there **is** time. God's Word counsels us, *"Seek the Lord while He may be found... Draw near to God and He will draw near to you... You will seek Me and find Me, when you search for Me with all your heart"* (Isaiah 55:6; James 4:8; Jeremiah 29:13). It is time to seek Him like never before on behalf of our families, our Church, and our nation. America's only hope is a pride-breaking, hell-shaking, life-altering revival, *and it will come if we will truly seek Him.*

3. Shaking can only remove what is "shakable;" the precious things will remain. And in the process, we will have our value system renewed by the Holy Spirit.

Our lives have become encumbered with many things—possessions, priorities, and pursuits that we do not need (and sometimes do not even want). These things tend to make our hearts look like many of our garages: cluttered and unfit for their intended use. The result is a heart unprepared for God's presence and fellowship. This time of shaking will help cleanse the temples of our lives, purging the proverbial dead branches from the tree, and allowing for fresh life to spring forth. It will give us a more eternal mindset, help us lose our appetite for this world's passing pleasures, and thus give us something of *genuine substance and worth* to offer the lost.

It may appear to be our nation's darkest day, yet it can also be the American Church's finest hour. If His people "humble themselves and pray," this season of shaking will lead to an unprecedented outpouring of His Spirit that will bring countless souls to salvation. However, it requires our cooperation.

Study the history of revival, and you will see an undeniable pattern: *revivals never start by majority vote, but by a remnant of praying people who refuse to accept anything less than a genuine move of God.*

It is time for God's people to lay hold of Him in prayer and not let go till the rains of His righteousness are flooding our nation and filling His Church.

Sow for yourselves righteousness;
Reap in mercy;
Break up your fallow ground,
For it is time to seek the LORD,
Till He comes and rains righteousness on you.

Hosea 10:12

Chapter 2

Missing: The Presence of God

GOD'S PEOPLE WERE ALWAYS INTENDED TO CARRY GOD'S PRESENCE. It is our birthright as Blood-bought children, our portion as His workers, and our witness to the world. Moses understood the primacy of God's presence when he said, "If Your presence does not go with us, do not send us up from this place" (Exodus 33:15).

If ancient Israel needed God's presence, the early Church needed it even more. She was born into a hostile world at a turbulent time, surrounded by foes both religious and political, and commissioned to proclaim the message of a risen Savior who was publicly crucified only weeks before.

In Luke 24 and Acts 1, Jesus gave His disciples a specific set of instructions:

1. **Wait** in Jerusalem;
2. **Receive** power;
3. *Then* **advance** My Kingdom.

For the disciples to ignore Jesus' progression would have been disastrous. There was no possibility of successfully carrying out Jesus' mission without Jesus' presence in the form of the indwelling Holy Spirit. This provided the power, boldness, direction, grace, and all else necessary to change the world in Jesus' Name.

Without God's presence, the disciples were a small, timid, powerless group of "average guys"—fishermen, blue-collar types, and even a reformed tax collector thrown in for good measure. They had no resources, no advertising budget, no name recognition, no training in church growth strategies, no worldly influence, and not one seminary degree between the whole lot of them. They were the most *improbable* group through which to birth the Church.

However, Acts 1 leads to Acts 2. Watch what happens when this same group of men receives the power of God in the presence of the Holy Spirit: they become bold (even fearless), eloquent in speech, irrefutable in preaching, powerful in word and mighty in deed. Observe Peter, the same man who only weeks before cowered before a servant girl as he thrice denied Jesus, now fearlessly preaching a message that could have gotten him killed. Watch as he single-handedly arrests the attention of Jews from all over the world, convicting their hearts, rebuking the whole of religious leadership in Jerusalem, and bringing some 3,000 Jewish souls to faith in the Messiah. This is the picture of a man *transformed by the presence of God!*

GOD'S WORK, GOD'S WAY

The early church set the pattern for us: doing God's work *necessitates* God's power and presence. There is simply no other way, no "plan B," no alternative power source. The early Church had no option but to obey Jesus' commands and wait, because to attempt God's work without God's presence and power would have been a guaranteed failure.

Why, then, is this our standard mode
of ministry operation today?
Why do human ingenuity and self-effort lie at
the core of so much of our religious effort?

*The American Church has been largely void of God's empow-
ering presence for so long that we are actually unaware of what
we lack.* Nearly 50 years ago A.W. Tozer wrote, **"The glory of
God has not been revealed to this generation of men."** We are
now at least two generations removed from the time when
God's people *expected* Him to dwell among us, to guide and
direct the Church, to empower ministry, and to inhabit our
praises. To many of us, the Book of Acts reads like a historical
account that has no relevance to the day in which we live. A
novice at history may consider the accounts of the American
Revolution to be interesting, but holding very little weight for
our lives today. It would appear that much of the Church has
come to see God's Word in a similar light.

In the absence of God's manifest Presence and demonstrated power, we have fashioned *golden calves:* traditions and
diversions designed to hold our attention and give us a sense
of comfort and decency about our religion. Consider:

- In the early Church, the focal point was the presence of
  the risen Christ; in the American Church, the focal point
  is the personality of the preacher in the pulpit.
- The early Church possessed real power to change lives
  and to free those enslaved to sin; the American Church
  adopts programs and support groups to help people
  cope with life and manage their sin.
- The early Church waited on God and moved according to
  His direction; the American Church doesn't have time to
  wait, but is constantly racing to stay "relevant" in a market-
  driven, me-centered culture. In the spirit of King Saul

who could not wait for Samuel's return *(1 Samuel 13)*, our worship is driven by the felt needs of the masses in the pews and the perceived desires of imagined "seekers." And our sacrifices are made in strict accordance to the morning service schedule (lest the people become impatient)!

yup!

- The early Church routinely experienced miracles, signs, and wonders—"demonstrations of the Spirit and of power" Paul called them—to confirm their preaching. In the American Church we have much preaching with little if any miraculous power (and no one wonders about it). The most important "signs" we possess are those handy and informative directional markers that guide first-time attendees to the visitor parking spots.

Quite seriously, if anything miraculous occurred in our typical American church service, it would be a source of utter shock and even disbelief. *We simply have no expectation that God will come with power when we gather together in His name.* And when the Spirit does attempt to interrupt our order of service with His presence and power, He is not always a welcome guest. The nature of man-made religious leadership is to distrust and dismiss what it cannot control.

- The early Church had the visible favor of Heaven, the undeniable attention of the world, and the focused hatred of hell. For all our crusades and outreaches, programs and pageantry, and for the countless millions of dollars in American church budgets, we know little of these three. Why? The answer is simple:

We *POSSESS* what the early Church *LACKED*,
and we *LACK* what the early Church *POSSESSED*.

"Silver and gold have I none, but such as I have give I thee." The early Church lacked worldly goods, resources, connections—

those things that lend a false sense of security and which easily become objects of our trust (i.e., idols).

If they were going to get the job done, it would require the presence of God. Today, we have ministry paraphernalia coming out of our ears, resources beyond description, a river of popular Christian books a mile wide (and a foot deep), and money enough to support every missionary in every nation on earth. Yet one thing we lack, and it is doubtless the better part: the power and presence of God.

One further thought on the vast material wealth of the American Church: "To whom much is given, much is required." Pastors, are we ready to answer to God for the way we have handled the mountain of resources He has entrusted to us?

RETURN TO THE PRESENCE

So what can we do? If we have lost God's presence as the focal point of our corporate and individual worship, how do we return? The answer is as clear for us as it was for the first group of disciples:

1. **Wait on God.** This means **surrendering** our wills and ways, **abandoning** our human means and methods, and **submitting** all we have and are to the lordship of Christ. This is a costly step, because it requires a resolute refusal to continue any longer in status quo American Christianity. Both for our personal lives and for our ministries, we must lay aside our ineffectual efforts, repent of our pride and misplaced trust, and wait on God for direction, wisdom, and power.

2. **Receive His power.** *God is more willing to supply than we are to receive.* He is well aware that every facet of the high calling He has given us—from walking in love and forgiving our foes, to making disciples and serving

in ministry—requires His help. Too often we *have* not because we *ask* not. We must ask (and keep asking) for the indwelling Presence of Christ in the person of the Holy Spirit. As we do, we will find the truth of Jesus' words, *"How much more will your heavenly Father give the Holy Spirit to those who ask."*

3. ***Then* advance His Kingdom.** Souls are at stake, eternity hangs in the balance, and countless millions are dying without Jesus' love. *We must cease playing church and return to the mission our Savior gave us to make disciples.* Recent statistics suggest that the average church in America is leading less than 2 people per year to faith in Christ. And of those numerical salvations, how many are really being made disciples? A generation of statistics reveals the answer... precious few.

One of the best-known evangelistic organizations in America has over a 90% "dropout rate." One year after a crusade, less than 10% of those who have "made a decision" are still going to church. Is this really what our Lord had in mind when He told us to make disciples? Or have we failed to "wait" and "receive" before we set out to reach the lost? Excellent marketing skills, name recognition, and huge budgets do not make disciples. Disciple making requires doing God's work God's way, *"teaching them to observe (obey) all things that I have commanded..."* (Matthew 28:20).

If we will return to God's ways, He will transform our lives and churches into a mighty witness for Him once more. The steps for us are simple, but powerful: **Wait... Receive... *then* Advance.** God will be more than faithful to do His part if we will do ours.

As Dr. Tozer aptly stated, **"We shall have as much success in Christian work as we have power, no more and no less."**

CHAPTER 3

American Worship: Twin Tragedies

THE OLD TESTAMENT GIVES US COUNTLESS EXAMPLES of what inevitably occurs when God's children fail to worship Him. It always results in worshiping something (or someone) else. God created humans to be worshipers, and we will by nature gravitate toward exalting someone or something.

> *Thou art worthy, O Lord,*
> *to receive glory and honor and power:*
> *for thou hast created all things,*
> *and FOR THY PLEASURE they are and were created.*
>
> Revelation 4:11 (KJV)

Amazingly, the Holy One who is continuously exalted in Heaven is still desirous of praises from mere mortals like you and me. Listen to Jesus' words:

But the hour is coming and now is,
when the true worshipers will worship
the Father in spirit and truth;
for THE FATHER IS SEEKING
SUCH TO WORSHIP HIM.

John 4:23

In the absence of giving God the glory He is due, Americans "celebrate" (worship) the "rich and famous"—athletes, celebrities, rock stars, cultural icons, political heroes, and most ironically of all, even well-known Christians. We seem hungry to ascribe greatness to something or someone beyond ourselves, a hunger that is designed to find its fulfillment only in the worship of the Creator.

TRAGEDY #1

The first great tragedy of worship in the modern American Church is this: following the spirit of the age, *we have made idols with our own set of celebrities and heroes,* especially preachers, authors, televangelists, Christian entertainers, and (perhaps worst of all) worship leaders. We have taken the praise and glory reserved for God alone and ascribed it, at least in part, to some of His workers—men and women of mere clay like the rest of us. My time on staff at a high-profile, 25,000 member "megachurch" gave me ample opportunity to experience this firsthand.

To display the absurdity of this trend in the American Church, let us turn the clock back several millennia. Imagine this scene taking place in ancient Israel during the time of the Solomonic Temple. The crowd of hundreds, maybe even *thousands* of Israelites are gathered for a worship extravaganza on the Temple grounds… the musicians are ready to rock the house… the menorahs are lit and the incense is wafting…

lambs are bleating, goats are annoying people, and bulls are doing whatever bulls do, as the people get ready to worship. Some of these Israelites have traveled a great distance for this event, and many have waited in line for hours just to get in the doors!

Then suddenly, a well-dressed man with a smart-looking beard (clearly hip to his generation) walks on stage to get things rolling: "People of God, are you ready to worship?!?" A roar from the crowd says "Yes!" "Hey, you guys look great today—and you sound great too! Well if you're ready to give it up for God, please welcome one of the most **dynamic, anointed worship leaders** of our day, whose sacrificial abilities are sought after all over Israel! Help me welcome, **the High Priest Baruch!!!**"

Baruch makes his entrance, knife in hand (for killing those poor sheepies), and the crowd goes berserk! With an electric atmosphere like this one, it's guaranteed to be some amazing worship, right?

Of course, this scene never took place in Israel. In fact, it is ludicrous. The focal point of the Temple was never supposed to be the priest; he was merely a necessary servant to help facilitate worship and instruct the people, and his personal charisma (or lack thereof) was inconsequential. If one priest dropped dead, another was ready to take his place, and worship continued according to God's plan.

No, the focal point of the Temple was **the presence of God.** That is what separated Israel from every other nation on earth, and it is what made their Temple sacred and their worship holy. ***The people of God are nothing without the presence of God.*** Moses' cry of, *"If Your presence does not go with us, do not bring us up from here,"* is just as true for us today. Without God's manifest presence, we are just "playing church," merely going through the motions of religious exercise—and it makes no difference whether our particular brand of church is more "charismatic" or "fundamentalist," liturgical or contemporary. Without God's presence, we are attempting to drive a car with no fuel in the tank.

WHAT ABOUT US?

The fictitious worship scene described was ludicrous, but no more so than what the American Church has done by glorifying pastors, preachers, evangelists, singers and worship leaders. It is just as silly, just as inexcusable, and just as idolatrous.

Consider this: why do Christians cheer when a worship leader/singer walks on stage? Why do they act like Brits in the presence of the Queen when they get the chance to meet a well-known preacher or author? Why do they wait in line for hours to purchase tickets to watch a "pastor" (motivational speaker) regurgitate the same self-help, feel-good, I'm-OK-you're-OK nonsense that he spoke at the last city on his nationwide tour? Are our lives really that small? *Or is our vision of God's glory so obscured,* our understanding of His power so diminished that we wrap our worship around whatever "golden calf" we can find?

Exodus 32 is one of the most profound chapters in Scripture regarding worship. In the preceding chapters the Israelites experienced mind-boggling displays of God's goodness, protection, provision and power on their behalf. God saved them at the Passover, caused them to plunder the Egyptians, took them through the Red Sea on dry land, drowned their foes in that very sea, made bitter waters sweet, sent bread from Heaven at dawn and quail on the evening winds, instructed them on how to live and worship, and gave them the constant sign of His presence in the pillar of cloud by day and fire by night. In a nutshell, Israel had it made.

And with all these miracles as a backdrop, they committed what is perhaps one of the most grievous sins in the entire Old Testament: they created a golden calf—formed from the very plunder God had secured for them—and declared it to be the god who delivered them from Egypt. Then, in a spirit of compromise and syncretism, Aaron proclaimed a feast to the LORD and the people began to "worship." First they ignored and offended God by creating a form and focus of worship entirely of their own making, and then they attempted to make it "OK" by calling the whole thing a feast to God:

> *Then they rose early on the next day,*
> *offered burnt offerings,*
> *and brought peace offerings;*
> *and the people sat down to eat and drink,*
> *and rose up to play.*

Exodus 32:6

TRAGEDY #2

This is the second great tragedy of worship in the American Church: *we have lost the manifest presence of God by creating worship in our own image*, making it whatever and however we want it to be. Modern worship is more influenced by trends of secular society than by God's Word, more informed by the opinions and whims of man than by the wisdom and desires of the Creator. I have known pastors with more fear of appearing "irrelevant" and out of touch with pop culture than *irreverent* to the Lord before whom they will stand on Judgment Day.

And to complete the tragic irony and inanity of our loss, we do not seem to be aware that we have lost anything. As long as the lights are on, the music is loud, and the sermon is smooth, the worshipers seem to be convinced that they have had the appropriate experience.

Weekend worship comes and goes and no one is changed; for we have been merely in the presence of man, heard only the words of man, sung songs written with the goal of moving only men's emotions. God is not truly sought, not welcomed, and not likely to show up because our "golden calf" is in the way. We do not see His glory anymore, and *we do not seem to know what we are missing.* Perhaps this explains why over seventy percent of churchgoers claim they have never experienced the presence of God in a worship service.

Oh my!

FROM THE HEART

This point is vital: the problem with American Church worship has little to do with the external form or program of our church services, and everything to do with the heart. Countless battles have been fought in churches to determine what worship should look like on the *outside*—"contemporary" vs. "traditional," guitars vs. organs, etc. This has created the painful irony of making worship—which should unite our hearts in adoration of our Savior—into a point of divisiveness and disunity. Rather than "showing preference in love" to one another and putting personal preference as last priority, many (both young and old) have done just the opposite, only steering our ship further from the presence of God.

No, the root of the problem with worship in the American Church is not in the external form, but **in the heart.** We have made worship about us—our likings, our preferences, our comfort, and our cultural expression. We worship our worship. *We have made the felt needs of man the rudder of our church worship experiences, and the result is the tragic loss of God's manifest Presence from our midst.*

TIME TO RETURN

So how do we return to Biblical worship? How do we cleanse the temples of our hearts and local churches so as to invite the Divine Presence whom we have grieved away? We must start by

28

repenting for the foolishness we have done in His name, and by submitting all we do and all we are to Him.

If we "rend our hearts, and not our garments" (Joel 2:13), He will guide us in how to bring Him a sacrifice that is pleasing to Him once again. All ministers (regardless of role or position) must ask:

1. Is the *GOAL* of my ministry that God alone be glorified and His people be strengthened?
2. Is the *MOTIVE* for my ministry a wholehearted love for the Savior and for His sheep?
3. Is the *FRUIT* of my ministry exalting and drawing all attention to Jesus? Or am I (even unintentionally) drawing attention to myself or to others? Do people leave corporate worship saying, "What a great God!" or "What a great minister!"?

We must take to heart the words of 19th century Scottish minister Robert Murray McCheyne:

> **"I see a man cannot be a faithful minister until he preaches Christ for Christ's sake, until he gives up striving to attract people to himself, and seeks only to attract them to Christ."**

While pastors have a great deal of responsibility in this process, *each of us* has a part to play in this restoration of pure worship in the American Church. We can do so through our prayers for our church leaders, through encouraging every *good* thing we see in our corporate worship times, and through offering loving correction in those areas where we fall short of the glory of God. And worship leaders, we must receive the correction and input offered us with an attitude of humility, love, and a teachable heart.

David sang, "Sacrifice and offering You did not desire; my ears You have opened." As we humble our hearts and yield our human agendas and man-centered ministry philosophies, God will open our ears to hear His will, for His Word says, "The humble He teaches His ways." He will restore to us a mantle of pure praise and pleasing worship if we will seek Him for it.

Then shall the Lord return "suddenly to His temple" *(Malachi 3:10)*, and our gatherings of worship will be alive with His manifest Presence once again. Therein lies the power to change lives, make disciples, heal the sick, set captives free, and draw the lost to the risen Savior.

When God is in our midst, the Church will have a genuine impact on the lost, for the world will marvel just as they marveled at Pentecost.

CHAPTER 4

America:
The Compromised Church

SATAN REALIZES THAT THE BEST WAY TO FIGHT the Church is from within.

Consider China, where Communism has attempted to snuff out the underground Church through a "full frontal assault," an all-out attack worthy of the Book of Acts. Yet from Satan's perspective, it has to be a huge disappointment. He set out to destroy a relatively small group of Christians, and instead they multiplied into a group of countless millions. Every time he imprisoned one of them, it seems that ten more rose up to take their place. If you are the devil, this is the definition of "backfire." China has proved what the history of martyrdom has long testified: you cannot kill the Church through open persecution, for the result will always be a stronger, more glorious Church.

It is unlikely that Satan has plans for such a frontal attack on the American Church (at least not yet). He realizes that the easiest way to marginalize the people of God is through the art of compromise, and his greatest allies are men who claim to speak in Jesus' Name.

Danger from Within

In chapters 23 and 24 of Numbers we see the futile attempts of Moab's wicked King Balak to defeat Israel through outside opposition in the form of outright cursing. He hires a prophet named Balaam, promising him great material gain if he will pronounce judgment and stir up the gods against God's people. The story becomes comical as the prophet-for-profit Balaam cannot seem to find anything bad to say about God's chosen ones. All of his attempts to curse turn into opportunities to bless, and God causes even attack to work together for the good of His people.

What Balak was unable to do to God's people from the outside, God's people managed to do to themselves. Israel invoked a self-inflicted curse by compromising a standard God had given them: no messing around with foreign women. Interestingly, Balaam was behind the scheme to have the Moabite women seduce the Israelite men into sexual sin *(see Numbers 31:16)*, which tells us something significant: when Satan fails to triumph through external attack, he simply goes inside the camp. The Israelites' greatest danger came not from without, but from the tendency to compromise within their own hearts.

Now, what could God possibly have against Moabite women that would make Him be so exclusive with His people? Simply this: God knew that foreign wives lead to foreign gods, that making covenant with the world leads to worshiping the world's ideas, ideals and idols. And it is no different for us today.

Israel ignored God's warning and suffered dearly for doing so as thousands lost their lives. And the moral of the story could not be any more poignant or timely for the American Church: compromise always starts with one small step, with ignoring one facet of God's instruction, and always leads to embracing the world's ways and worship. And unless repented of quickly, compromise always ends in needless pain and destruction, and ultimately in separation from God and His presence.

CT—Compromise Today

In just one generation, evangelical pastors and ministry leaders have sabotaged the Church's future by abandoning the faith of our past. In our lust for acceptance and validation by the culture, we have traded timeless, eternal truth for humanistic and relativistic ideals. Consider the Biblical pillars we have downplayed, minimized, or even omitted in our frantic attempts to make Christianity more palatable or "culturally relevant:"

- The anointed teaching of **God's Word.** We have gone from meat to milk… to formula;
- Preaching the reality and consequences of **sin.** The mere mention of sin is deemed insensitive or distasteful;
- Preaching true **repentance** as a prerequisite for salvation;
- The unapologetic proclamation of the **Blood of Christ** as the only means of atonement and redemption;
- **Discipleship** as the normal Christian life, not just for missionaries and the super-spiritual;
- Taking up our **cross** (a life of self-denial) as the expectation of all Believers;
- **Suffering** as a prerequisite for glory;
- The **power of the Holy Spirit** as a normative and indispensable part of every Christian's life, and the only source of true power for **victorious living;**
- Real **fellowship** (think "friendship") with other Believers as a necessity for a healthy church and healthy Christians;

⊙ Our calling to live a **sanctified** life, one that is set apart
  for God's will and ways;
◐ Growing in God's **holiness.**

DOES GOD STILL CARE ABOUT THAT HOLINESS THING?

Holiness is a term so misrepresented and maligned in our
society that the Church has largely retreated from using it. Not
surprisingly, we have made a pretty impressive retreat from
practicing it as well.

God repeatedly calls us throughout scripture to be "sanctified;" literally, "set apart." Before our heads swim with images
of monasteries and self-righteous Pharisees, we must recognize that God's call to be sanctified is anything but a futile cycle
of powerless self-effort. The sanctified life that Jesus requires
has its eyes on the One *to* whom it is set apart, not on the
world *from* which it is set apart. This is not the phony, "Sunday
best," smile-because-the-pastor-is-watching facade of holiness
that we have grown accustomed to in the American Church.
Rather, it is a Spirit-empowered holiness that exalts Christ and
thus draws the lost to the Savior.

Because holiness has gotten a bad rap of late, we have
devised other methods in the American Church to reach the
hypothetical "seeker."

Many fruitless schemes have been devised to reach the lost
through becoming more like them in lifestyle, entertainment,
dress, mindset, etc. *(think "seeker-sensitive")*. And what do we
have to show for our efforts?

- Historic lows in church attendance, cultural impact, and
  societal transformation;
- All-time highs in church divorce rates, pornography use
  and addiction, prayerlessness, powerlessness, and true
  irrelevance to the nation where God has placed us;

Jesus walked the earth in absolute holiness and utter sin-lessness, yet think of how notoriously sinful people related to Him. *They were drawn to genuine holiness.* You and I are not Jesus, and no doubt we fall far short of His perfection. But *God can take the imperfect life that is wholly surrendered to Him and make it a reflection of His holiness,* with the genuine power, mercy and love that a lost world is dying to know.

A CALL TO RETURN

For the Church to return to her rightful place of Godly influence and authority, she must be unafraid to lovingly and boldly preach the fullness of God's Word once more, without apology. But before we can do that with authority, we must be people who are *personally, passionately in love with Jesus Christ.* This means recognizing and confessing every way in which we have neglected our "First Love," repenting for our sin, forsaking our idols (those distractions and selfish pursuits we have allowed to fill our hearts and lives), and making our friendship with God the first priority of our lives. Anything less is mere emotionalism and will never produce genuine revival.

The needed repentance must touch both pulpit and pew, for each of us has been a part of the problem (and thus can be a part of God's solution). Personal repentance invites the Spirit's presence, for He is drawn to brokenness and genuine humility:

> *For thus say the High and Lofty One*
> *Who inhabits eternity, whose name is Holy:*
> *"I dwell in the high and holy place,*
> *WITH HIM WHO HAS A CONTRITE AND*
>   *HUMBLE SPIRIT,*
> *To revive the spirit of the humble,*
> *And to revive the heart of the contrite ones."*
>
> Isaiah 57:15

35

As you and I repent of our sins and turn our hearts toward our Father, the Spirit strikes a flame of personal revival in our individual lives; yet His flame seldom stops there, because *personal revival often begets corporate revival.* Your repentance and fresh pursuit of God can have an exponential effect on the Church as God uses your life and prayers to impact those around you with their need for revival as well.

Whatever your place in the Body of Christ, *you have a vital part to play in the awakening that is so desperately needed.*

Let us seek God like never before.

CHAPTER 5

New Cross, No Cross

THE "OLD CROSS" VERSUS THE "NEW CROSS" was a phenomenon that troubled A.W. Tozer in the mid-twentieth century. His concern was that although Christians of his day talked much about the Cross, what they meant by that term was something radically different than what Scripture shows the Cross to be. The "new cross" did not have the call to discipleship, the denying oneself, and the laying down of one's life for others that Jesus taught and embodied. The "old cross" was concerned with the glory of God at all costs, while the "new cross" was concerned primarily with one's own happiness.

Tozer's assessment of the mid-20th century Church has proved all too accurate, which makes one wonder what he would have to say to *our* generation were he here to see it. For instead of being a church with a "new cross," we have become a church with "no cross."

"Not so!" you may be thinking. *"We've got a cross hanging behind the pulpit, one hanging on the front of the building—we've*

even got one in the gymnasium!" But the cross which we now discuss resides not on the wall, but rather in the preaching, worship, and evangelism of the local church. This is a crucial issue because *as goes our emphasis on the Cross, so goes our presentation of the Gospel.* Oswald Chambers wrote, "Every doctrine not embedded in the Cross of Jesus will lead astray," and we now have a host of such doctrines in the American Church.

THE ORIGINAL GOSPEL

The Cross was the centerpiece of the Gospel of the early Church. The apostles preached as Jesus had taught them, carrying forth "the Gospel of the Kingdom" *(Matthew 24:14)*. As demonstrated in the Book of Acts and as taught in the epistles, this Gospel included:

- Repenting of (confessing and turning from) sin;
- The crucified Savior as God's instrument of redemption;
- Forgiveness of sins by His Blood;
- Salvation by faith in Jesus' Name (and none other);
- Baptism as an act of obedience to Christ's command and a sign of consecrating one's life;
- Signs and wonders as a normal part of evangelism (healing, for instance);
- The casting out of demons; and
- The power of the Holy Spirit as a normative experience for all who have believed.

While the evangelical Church of recent history has not experienced much of genuine miracles, signs, and wonders, evangelical churches **were** once strong when preaching repentance, forgiveness by the Blood, salvation by faith, and the atoning work of Jesus accomplished at the Cross. In historic American evangelicalism, preachers *preached* the Cross, hymnals contained songs to help us *sing* the Cross, and churchgoers generally understood that without Jesus' death on the Cross we would all be helplessly, hopelessly lost. This was one of the greatest strengths of the evangelical Church.

And yet in this last generation, the American Church has squandered this precious inheritance of Biblical doctrine regarding the Cross, turning instead to a "golden calf" of self-made doctrinal ingenuity. We have pulled from the fire a "crossless" gospel: a low impact, non-offensive, easy-listening version of the real thing, the theological equivalent of elevator music.

ARE WE SMARTER THAN THE APOSTLE PAUL?

"Why on earth would preachers cease preaching the Cross?" you might be asking. The answer is simple: in our age of political correctness and in our lust for acceptance, preachers are abandoning the Cross *because it offends people.* Paul himself stated that whether Jew or Gentile, the Cross finds a way to offend the pride of every variety of human being *(see 1 Corinthians 1:22-23).*

Why is the Cross offensive to humanity? It is offensive because it presents us with the reality of how greatly our sin offends a holy God. It reminds us of the unfathomable price He paid to save us, and therefore how utterly devoted and yielded we should be to Him *(Romans 12:1-2).*

The Cross means personal responsibility for our sins and personal accountability to live for Jesus, because we are no longer our own. We "were bought at a price" by our Savior's blood *(1 Corinthians 6:19-20).*

But today, we have found a way around the offense of the Cross: we simply do not preach it. In an age of rampant individualism and unbridled self-centeredness, the seeker-sensitive influence within the Church has accommodated the culture's felt need for validation by omitting the central theme of Paul's preaching, and has replaced it with man-centered religion designed to help people feel better about themselves. Hence, the focus has shifted from being *saved* from sin to being **healed** from the consequences of sin.

LEFT BEHIND BY THE CHURCH

Sadly, the Cross is not the only element of the historic evangelical Gospel that we have recently left behind. Let me describe the new "gospel" that is becoming increasingly prevalent in the American Church of our day:

- The new gospel omits the **Cross** (already discussed);
- The new gospel omits the **Blood.** This is because surveys have (supposedly) shown that "seekers" do not like the whole concept of "blood," especially not as a means of washing away sin. They presumably want something a bit tidier.

Absurd? Yes, but it is really, truly happening in the Church today, and not only amongst the liberal or mainline denominations, either. A friend of mine was serving at an historic Southern Baptist church a few years ago. His role was as worship director for their new "contemporary" worship service, which they were advertising as being *"Real, Rocking, and Relevant."* Hmm… The basic premise was that the 50-something-year-old pastor would attempt to appear a bit more "hip" by abstaining from wearing a tie, and would preach shorter messages with less Scripture (more stories) so as to reach the mythological and elusive "seeker."

One Sunday morning my friend was preparing the worship team to handle the "Rocking" part of the equation when Pastor Relevant approached him about his song selections for the morning:

"Umm… what's that you're singing?" he asked.

"The Blood Medley," my friend replied. "You know, like, hymns about the Blood… um, 'Nothing but the Blood of Jesus,' you know… hymns?" My friend assumed that the problem was the style in which the songs were being put across, perhaps a bit more "rocking" than they had bargained for. But the pastor quickly cleared up any confusion.

"Umm… yeah, that's the problem…aaahhh, seeee, ummmm, well, **we don't like to mention the Blood here—it offends people.**" And he ordered my friend to scratch those hymns from the worship service at this historic church.

What would Spurgeon say? A Baptist church afraid to sing hymns about the Blood of Christ for fear of offending the lost? Unthinkable! But this is just one of countless real-life examples of the violence being done to the Gospel of Jesus Christ all across our nation. We have a crossless, bloodless gospel; but the madness does not stop there.

- The new gospel gives no mention of **sin** *(which would necessitate talking about the Cross and the Blood)*. "Sin" has been replaced with the terms "mistakes" or "poor decisions," both of which sound harmless enough, and certainly less indicting. While it is true that we all make both mistakes and poor decisions, neither of those will send us to hell—but sin will.

"Mistakes" and "poor decisions" can leave us feeling like innocent victims of an imperfect human nature, stuck in the same boat as every other well-meaning, basically nice person on planet earth. "Hey, cut me some slack! I mean, *everybody* makes mistakes, right?" But "sin" carries a definite and inescapable sense of personal responsibility for moral wrongs against a holy God, resulting in consequences both temporal and eternal, and leaving us with the desperate awareness of our need for a Savior.

Simply put, *awareness of sin leads to awareness of need, leading to salvation.* And failure to talk about sin in efforts to not offend the "seeker" is foundational insanity. *How will we answer on the Day of Judgment when real souls are bound to an eternity in a very real hell because (in part) we were afraid to talk about real sin?*

- The reality of **hell** is another scripturally irrefutable and essential element of the Gospel that has sadly fallen out of vogue in the American Church. The reason is the same: we do not want to offend. We are convinced that seekers do not want to think of a God who would "send people to hell" for their sins.

ALL NICE PEOPLE GO TO HEAVEN?

Remarkably, the American Church's fastest growing notion regarding hell is not found in the Bible at all. Instead, it is an idea we have borrowed from "inclusivism." Inclusivism is a liberal impostor of genuine Christianity which teaches in essence that "God loves everybody; He's too nice to send anyone to hell, it's just a metaphor anyway, so let's just not talk about it, because what matters most is that we're all nice people and have a happy life," etc. This "doctrine" is simply New Age teaching with a paper-thin veneer of Christian terminology glazed over the top. And yet this is eerily close to the "gospel" being preached by some of the most popular Christian television celebrities in some of the most successful (numerically speaking) megachurches in America.

Thankfully, some people truly *can* see through the silliness. I was interviewing for a pastoral position several years ago at a large conservative church. The pastor and I were getting to know each other over a cup of coffee, and he was intrigued to find out that I had been on staff at a church that he regularly watched on television. "It's a good show, and that preacher sure has a great stage presence," he said politely. "But, umm," he hesitated, his voice lowering so no one in the coffee shop would overhear his next question, "isn't his message a little… *New Age?*" Exactly.

Who Goes to Hell?

Christians often struggle with how to handle questions regarding the reality and purpose of "hell," especially when talking with an unbeliever. The answer is a simple one: *let Scripture speak for itself.* The New Testament gives a straightforward response in three clear points:

1. Hell was not prepared by God for people, only "for the devil and his demons" *(Matt. 25:41)*;
2. It is "not His will that any should perish" (thus be sent to hell) but rather "that all should receive eternal life" *(2 Peter 3:9)*;
3. Therefore man sends **himself** to hell by sinning, and then rejecting the forgiveness of sins offered through Jesus' shed Blood on the Cross *(John 3:17-18)*.

Last But Not Least, Ignoring the Spirit of God

- The last vital Biblical element that is commonly missing from mainstream American Church teaching (and experience) is **the presence of the Holy Spirit in our daily life** to guide, comfort, empower over sin, and help us bear good fruit for God's glory.

In John chapters 14-16, Jesus placed tremendous prominence on the Holy Spirit's role in the life of those who would follow Him. The rest of the New Testament bears this out, as we are exhorted to walk in the Spirit, to be led by the Spirit, to bear the fruit of the Spirit, to overcome sin by the Spirit, to be renewed by the Spirit, and so forth. **Biblically speaking, it is nearly impossible to overstate the essentiality of the Spirit's role in the lives of God's people.**

Yet the Holy Spirit has been made into something of an enigma in the modern American Church. At times this is due to a lack of right Biblical teaching about the Spirit, which has produced fear and misunderstanding among God's people. Tozer wrote that he witnessed among churchgoers "a hardness of heart caused by hearing men without the Spirit constantly preaching about the Spirit." It would appear that the Church today has suffered from such teaching.

At other times, the strange behavior and bad fruit of those who claim to be "directed by the Spirit" (while truly in the flesh) has caused others to fear the Spirit's presence. There has been much done in the name of the Spirit of God for which the Spirit would take no inspiration, ownership, nor responsibility. The sad effect among some Christians is a fear and wariness of the Spirit's work, as the counterfeit has stolen their appetite for the genuine article.

But quite often, *we lack the Holy Spirit simply because we have ignored Him.* We are so busy with our powerless, man-centered, agenda-driven programs and meetings that we have left no room for the Divine Presence. We choose our efforts over His power, the personality of men over the presence of the Spirit, and religious busyness over waiting on God.

No Spirit, No Power; No Power, No Victory

Our lack of Biblical emphasis on the Spirit is perhaps most vividly illustrated in the widespread *powerlessness over sin* amongst Christians today. Millions of American churchgoers' lives are a ceaseless struggle to avoid sin, accomplished (they hope) with the tools of good intentions and the weapons of self-effort. Missing from this equation is the power of God's Spirit to lead us in right paths, to warn us of temptation and danger, to renew our minds according to God's Word, to transform our hearts, and to empower us to crucify the flesh.

GOD'S PATH FOR A VICTORIOUS LIFE

Paul tells us that "if *BY THE SPIRIT* you put to death the deeds of the body, you will live" *(Romans 8:13). Every step of victory must be accomplished through the power of the Spirit of God,* or it will prove to be short-lived at best and counter-productive at worst. No matter how sincere and well-meaning one may be, *all the good efforts in the world will not keep you from falling into temptation.* **A holy life necessitates the power of the Holy Spirit.** While we *cooperate* with the Spirit through our steps of obedience (such as spending time in His Word, asking for His help daily, and avoiding areas of temptation), *the power* to grow in His holiness is always and entirely His alone. And the *motivation* is solely a response of love to the One who saved us, never a legalistic attempt to earn His favor or prove our own righteousness.

In this manner, the more we grow in true obedience to Him, the *less* likely we are to take credit for any victory or growth, since we are thoroughly aware that every step is the result of His Spirit's power and presence in our lives. And God *desires* to teach us how to walk in His Spirit, to abide in His friendship, and to grow in obedience to His Word and will.

This life in the Spirit makes growing in God's holiness a *joy*—for it keeps the focus on our friendship with Him. *We no longer strive under a heavy burden of self-effort, but walk in the knowledge of His love and allow His Spirit to provide what only He can.* If this sounds too good to be true, then realize that our lack of experiencing God's Word can actually dull our ability to receive the truths therein. The problem is never with God's promises, nor with God's power. The problem arises when our doctrine and experience have fallen so far short of Biblical Christianity that we no longer believe the promises God has made us as His Blood-bought children. *And if we fail to believe God's promises, we rob them of their effectual power in our lives.*

REAL RIGHTEOUSNESS BY SIMPLE FAITH

Even the Gospel itself has no power in the heart that will not believe *(see Hebrews 4:2)*. Think back to how you received salvation: was it through any effort or goodness of your own? On the contrary, you *heard* the promise of God, and *responded* with faith *(even a mustard seed was enough to begin with)*, thus *believing* and *receiving* what God had promised. In essence, you *agreed* with God's Word and responded with childlike faith. And the result was the greatest transformation imaginable, as you were translated from the kingdom of darkness into the Kingdom of His Son, to love and serve Him in this life and to enjoy His presence for all eternity. All the necessary power was supplied by the Blood of Christ and the Spirit of God; your part was to believe and respond.

Here, then, is some of the best news any sincere, struggling Christian could possibly hear (and I pray that you receive this truth into the depth of your heart): **our practical experience of God's *righteousness* comes the same way as our practical experience of His *salvation*—BY FAITH.** All the power to overcome sin is supplied by the Blood of Christ to cleanse us, the Word of God to renew our minds, and the Spirit of God to lead, empower, and transform us. Our part is to *believe* and *respond.*

Just as the miracle of salvation came as a result of *childlike faith,* God's holiness comes to our lives in *exactly the same manner,* by the very same means. As we agree with Scripture, His Spirit begins to change us *on the inside,* for "the Word of God effectively works in you who believe" *(1 Thessalonians 2:13b).*

In the light of this glorious truth, consider with fresh faith just a few of the exceedingly precious promises God has made to you as His child: *sin no longer has dominion over you,* for you are not under the power of the law, but under the grace of God *(Romans 6:14).* Just as surely as Christ was made to be sin for you, God has called you "the righteousness of God in

Christ Jesus" *(2 Corinthians 5:21)*. You possess a righteousness not built upon self-effort, but a *real* righteousness that is *from God* and *through faith* in Christ Jesus *(Philippians 3:9)*. You are (right now, this very moment) a "new creation" in Christ, learning to walk in the power of His Spirit more and more each day *(2 Corinthians 5:17; Galatians 5:16)*. You are freed by the Spirit of God from serving sin and death *(Romans 8:2)*, and free to obey your Savior, for "if the Son makes you free, you shall be free indeed" *(John 8:36)*. You are *led and empowered* by the Holy Spirit *(Romans 8:13-14)*, and are more than a conqueror over everything the devil, the flesh, and the world can send against you *(Romans 8:35-39)*. Furthermore, you are set free from all shame, accusation, and condemnation by the Blood of the Lamb *(Romans 8:1, 33-34)*, as you forget what lies behind (including all your past sins) and you press on to know, love, and serve Jesus with all you are *(Philippians 3:12-14)*. *This is who you are in Christ, and how God sees you.* And **the more you believe these promises, the more you will see them effectively working in your life.**

SUMMING UP

In essence, the "gospel" becoming increasingly popular in the American Church today lacks a right teaching of and emphasis on the Cross, the Blood, the truths of sin and hell, and the power of the Holy Spirit unto a victorious life. We must ask ourselves: what is left?

Perhaps you are wondering why we should make such a commotion about these issues. After all, is it really so important what we preach, as long as we are speaking a positive, hope-filled message that helps the listener become a better person and (most importantly) live a happy, purposeful life?

The crux of the matter is that **the gospel becoming prevalent in 21ˢᵗ century American Christianity is not just a variation on** the message Jesus entrusted to us; *it is a different gospel altogether.* About such things, Paul wrote:

> *But even if we, or an angel from heaven,*
> *preach any other gospel to you than*
> *what we have preached to you,*
> *let him be accursed.*

Galatians 1:8

RETURN TO THE REAL THING

It is crucial that the Church return to preaching *and living* the Gospel as demonstrated in Scripture. As we enter into the final season of America's history, *the only hope our nation has is a spiritual awakening—a revival of Biblical proportions.* This will never happen unless we are preaching God's Word in God's love, under God's anointing, without excuse and without apology. Warren Wiersbe wrote, "Our nation is desperately in need of spiritual awakening. But our emphasis on evangelism apart from doctrine will certainly not do it."

God's Spirit will never fall with holy fire upon an altar of human ingenuity or a golden calf of popular ideas. We must return to the true Gospel; therefore, we must restore the Cross as the centerpiece of our theology, preaching, and experience. Only in the Cross do we see the full passion of a perfect God to rescue and redeem a rebellious humanity. Only in the Cross do we see the full extent of the Father's love for our souls.

Proponents of a crossless, bloodless gospel may be well-intentioned. They may genuinely desire to be "sensitive to the seekers." But in reality, such a misguided message fails to love the lost by failing to present the truth. The tragedy is that such a sham of a gospel will send men to hell while thinking they are saved.

CHAPTER 6

Purpose or Passion?

THERE WAS A GREAT FAD AFOOT in Christendom in recent times. Churches everywhere were describing themselves as being "*purpose-driven.*" Tired of being adrift in a sea of purposelessness, thousands of churches (and millions of churchgoers) signed up to ride the wave of personal fulfillment on a journey "driven" by purpose. Some pastors called it a "move of God," likening it to a revival. Moreover, the secular press *loved* the book, receiving its ideas warmly and promoting it with enthusiasm. Christ said that the world would hate the truth, hate the Church, and hate true disciples; but they certainly loved this book!

Now, several years later, the fad is fading. The purpose-driven party is over, and the books and video series have made their way to the bargain table at your local, friendly Christian bookstore. And what have we gained for the experience? *What is the net effect on the American Church?*

My purpose is not to bash anyone's book, nor their marketing campaign. (*Did you buy the purpose-driven desk calendar?*)

Whenever anyone is helped in their walk with God, we should rejoice. God constantly uses imperfect means and ministers because He is a merciful God, and imperfect vessels are the only type available. Furthermore, there are some true (albeit basic) statements in the purpose-driven books and curriculums, and if some Christians were genuinely encouraged, thank God.

What purpose-driven ideology lacked in Biblical substance and depth it attempted to make up for with *marketing genius.* It accurately identified that 21st century churches are largely lethargic, their preachers powerless, and their churchgoers disinterested with the ceaseless stream of programs offered them. Pastors are tired of feeling irrelevant and ignored by mainstream culture, and churchgoers are wondering what on earth they are supposed to be doing with their lives.

"Purpose-driven" seemed to have all the answers, starting with the premise that *"it's not all about you."* "Amen!" Any true follower of Christ will concur. And then the book proceeded to teach *just the opposite,* for in purpose-driven ideology, your journey IS all about you: **your** purpose, to fulfill **your** life, to be the best **you** can be.

In this mindset, our lives are "driven" **not** by a passion for God's glory, but by a pursuit of personal purpose carried out in good works—with the focus still on self-realization and personal fulfillment. Scripture tells the new Believer to *"carry your cross,"* while this best-selling book told him or her to *"pursue your purpose."* And so their paths diverge.

This is a vital point, because the me-centered philosophy that made "purpose-driven" so popular is foundational to the ideology of the modern megachurches: *God's highest purpose for man is personal fulfillment, individual happiness, and that each of us enjoys a sense of achievement.* And the evidence of God's blessing is growth in numbers through the door and dollars in the budget, not in disciples made. It is like having an Olympic-sized swimming pool with no deep end, just "shallow" and "shallower." You may have built it 75 feet wide, but it is still only 2 feet deep.

Fads die fast. Five years later, few of us really cared about the answers provided by the purpose-driven products, and the American Church moved on to find new programs. Why? The answer is found in Isaiah chapter 40:

> *All flesh is grass, and all its loveliness is like*
> *the flower of the field…*
> *The grass withers, the flower fades,*
> *but THE WORD OF OUR GOD STANDS FOREVER.*
>
> Isaiah 40:6,8

All religious exercise and effort that has the happiness of man as its highest goal is like the grass and flower described by Isaiah. It may appear beautiful for a season, but will be short-lived. It possesses no staying power because it is based on nothing deeper than the pursuit of our own happiness. When the storms of life hit (as they invariably do), such man-centered ideas offer nothing of substance with which to weather the storm, even when wrapped in a veneer of Scripture.

THE BOOK HE NEVER WROTE

Let us contrast the purpose-driven fad with another book that can also boast millions of copies sold: *My Utmost for His Highest* by Oswald Chambers. This book was a compilation of sermons and teachings that Chambers gave in a small Bible school in England, and in YMCA huts in Egypt during WWI as he ministered to soldiers (not exactly glamorous or high-profile locations for writing a book).

Unlike some of today's Christian mega-leaders, Oswald never pastored a megachurch, never sought (or found) great commercial success, never counseled important politicians, never attempted to unite churchgoers with other world religions to solve all of humanity's problems, and never made a huge fortune in the ministry. And in fact, Chambers never set out to write this book. His wife assembled the teachings after his death. (He passed away at the age of 43 from complications following a surgery). The messages contained therein are not a series of slick ideas. They are more like a volley of punches coming from a veteran prize fighter. And Chambers truly pulls no punches. He preaches like a man whose sole passion is to glorify Christ and to help others do the same.

And now, over 70 years after its initial publishing in America, why is *My Utmost* still the best-selling devotional of all time? Because it gives more than shallow answers and man-centered ideology; rather, it gives the meat of God's Word under the anointing of the Holy Spirit. Countless men and women of God over the decades have marveled that Chambers seemed to be preaching to their personal circumstances, shedding the light of Scripture on their very areas of individual need. How can this be? Because this book was from the heart of God, not the mind of man. And it came through a yielded vessel, *a servant of God who possessed a passion for His glory.*

Therein lies the crux of the matter: **our lives were never intended to be lived in pursuit of purpose, but rather in pursuit of God Himself.** Living with a passion for God's glory is the only calling worthy of Jesus' sacrifice for us. Such a life is distinctly God-centered, concerned with His glory alone, and will be surely attended with His power.

PASSION BEATS PURPOSE, EVERY TIME

The season of shaking has begun, and life is becoming increasingly difficult for more Americans. It is vital that God's people have the rock of His unchanging love beneath their feet, that their faith is built upon His unfailing Word, and that they know beyond a shadow of a doubt for Whom they are living. The pursuit of purpose will prove powerless in such a season of shaking, but a passion for God's glory will prove to be a source of strength and clarity amid turbulent times.

For those Christians still trying to be "driven by purpose," realize that *purpose is transient in all our lives*—life necessitates transition, dreams die, and seasons change. Building your life on purpose will prove an elusive and frustrating exercise, because purpose will prove fickle. However, *a passion for God's glory will never fail the child of God*. It remains the highest calling, the worthiest pursuit, and the grandest goal through life's passing seasons.

Furthermore, *good doctrine (the right teaching of God's Word) works everywhere and in every situation*. Consider our brothers and sisters in the Suffering Church, in places like China or North Korea. How would they apply purpose-driven ideology? How would someone who is imprisoned for their faith and enduring daily beatings for the sake of Christ find "purpose" in their life that helps them feel special and important to God and others? That sounds absurd because it is. The self-centered American fad of purpose is as useless to the Suffering Church as is the gospel of greed so often marketed by the "health and wealth" churches.

However, that Chinese brother can identify with the Apostle Paul who suffered imprisonment and beatings for the glory of Christ. He can rejoice with Paul that whether by life or by death, Christ will be glorified in his body (*Philippians 1:20*). And a passion for God's glory will carry our brother through even the cruelest torture and persecution as he shares in the fellowship of Christ's sufferings (*Philippians 3:10*). Knowing that sharing in Jesus' sufferings leads to sharing in His glory (*Romans 8:17*), he can even consider such intense trials to be "light" and "momentary" when compared at the "far more exceeding and eternal weight of glory" which awaits (*2 Corinthians 4:17*). A life lived for God's glory will bear fruit even in the harshest surroundings, because *God visits such a life with His power.* And such a life is never, ever lived in vain.

Oswald Chambers died young, leaving behind a grieving wife and daughter. To the natural mind, it seemed a waste—so much potential for greatness, but so little "success." Yet he lived his life for God's glory, his "utmost for God's highest," and God has subsequently made his life a blessing and inspiration to countless millions of Christians over seven decades. And *his* book never, ever winds up on the bargain table of your local friendly Christian bookstore. Passion beats purpose, every time.

RETURN TO THE RIGHT PURSUIT

I encourage you: make the pursuit of your life to love, honor, and glorify your Savior in all you do and in all you are. Surrender your rights, goals, dreams, *even your life itself* to the One who died for you, and trust that He will guide you in His highest will for your life. Pursue Him first and foremost, *seeking "first the Kingdom of God and His righteousness."* Your Father will grant all you need to give God your utmost for His highest.

Live with passion for God's glory, not for your purpose.

CHAPTER 7

Cheap Grace, Easy Believism, and Self-Love

FREE GRACE AND UNCONDITIONAL LOVE, accessible to all mankind by simply reciting the "sinner's prayer," has been the "gospel" championed by the American Church for decades. To modern Christianity, successful evangelism looks like a stadium of people hearing a "salvation message" and responding by making their way to the front of the building, repeating what the speaker says, and then being told, *"Congratulations! You're a Christian!"* This teaching and method has near universal acceptance in the evangelical Church, *but is it Biblical?*

Tozer wrote, "the emotionless act of 'accepting the Lord' practiced among us bears little resemblance to the whirlwind conversions of the past." If he was right, and our methodology of evangelism is lacking God's intended transforming power, then we are setting converts up for a life of powerless, nominal Christianity from the very start.

Our modern idea of evangelism is based on our definitions of "grace," "believing in Christ" (getting saved), and "unconditional love." Let us examine the way the Church has come to understand these terms and see if they align with God's Word.

AMAZING GRACE

Amazingly, some of the most popular notions regarding grace in the Church today are not to be found in Scripture. At best, grace resides in our doctrine as the indistinguishable twin brother of mercy. At worst, grace is our justification for habitual sin and deadly strongholds that guarantee our continued lack of spiritual power.

In modern American Christianity, the words "grace" and "mercy" have become nearly interchangeable. Ask a seminarian to define "grace," and he will likely say, "Unmerited favor," because that is what he has been taught. Then ask him to define "mercy," and he may pause: "Hmm... well, it's a lot like grace."

To help give us a fuller picture of the Biblical concept of grace, consider this excerpt from the Strong's Concordance definition: "grace...the merciful kindness by which God, *EXERTING HIS HOLY INFLUENCE upon souls, turns them to Christ, keeps, STRENGTHENS, INCREASES them in Christian faith, knowledge, affection, and KINDLES THEM TO THE EXERCISE OF THE CHRISTIAN VIRTUES*" (emphasis mine).

Modern Church teaching has watered down grace to mean merely "forgiveness when I sin," thus robbing us of much of the meaning and effectual working of God's grace in our lives. Truly, God's grace is unmerited (a free, unearned, and undeserved gift), and forgiveness is one vital expression of His grace toward us. However, Biblically speaking, *grace is far more than forgiveness alone!*

Consider the Lord's response to the Apostle Paul when he "pleaded with the Lord three times" that his "thorn in the flesh" be removed. ***My grace is sufficient for you, for My power is*** *made perfect in weakness,*" the Lord replied *(2 Corinthians 12:9).* If grace only means "forgiveness" then God's reply missed the mark, for Paul was not requesting atonement, but rather deliverance from a specific (though unspecified), protracted trial. However, God promised Paul *all that he needed* to overcome the battle: His grace. And notice that the Lord's response immediately tied His *grace* to His *power.*

God's Joy, Our Strength

In the Greek language (in which the New Testament was written), "*grace*" comes from the same root word as "*joy*" and "*gift.*" With this in mind, when one examines "grace" in the context of its uses in Scripture, this statement can be inferred: *Biblical grace is a gift of God's joy that strengthens us in time of need, helping us endure trials and overcome temptations through Christ.* That grace empowers us to overcome temptation is clearly shown in Hebrews 4:15-16 (and notice the distinctions made between grace and mercy):

> *For we do not have a High Priest*
> *who cannot sympathize with our weaknesses,*
> *but was in all points tempted as we are,*
> *   yet without sin.*
> *Let us therefore come boldly to the throne of grace,*
> *that we may OBTAIN MERCY and*
> *FIND GRACE TO HELP IN TIME OF NEED.*
>
> Hebrews 4:15-16

Far from giving us an excuse to sin, Biblical grace empowers us to overcome sin. Again, from Tozer: "*It is not the teaching of the Scriptures that grace makes us free to do evil. Rather, it sets us free to do good.*" God's grace makes us strong, sets us free, and leads us to experience His victory over sin, for as Paul wrote, "Sin shall not have dominion over you, for you are not under law but *UNDER GRACE*" *(Romans 6:14).*

In pastoral work, I have had young Christians tell me, "Hey, that's what grace is all about," when attempting to justify and excuse patterns of compromise, spiritual laziness, and habitual sin in their lives. Where did they get this idea? Tragically, much contemporary Church teaching has cheapened our under-standing of God's grace till it becomes mere license, something to be trampled with our compromise and complacency. And many popular evangelical authors have (whether intentionally or unwittingly) propagated this falsehood through their best-selling books.

REAL GRACE, REALLY AMAZING

A widely-read Christian book from the 1990's asked us to consider what was so amazing about grace, and devoted chapters to the answer without ever touching on true Biblical grace. Another best-selling author mistakenly defines grace as simply "the freely given and unmerited favor and love of God," charging that the Church has "twisted the gospel of grace into religious bondage," apparently unaware that his books are in danger of twisting true grace into license for sin. Millions read of "scandalous grace" that excuses a life of disobedience, while a more recent best-selling storyteller describes enjoying "the wastefulness of grace" in his own life. Each of these arrive at the popular but false notion that grace is an excuse for sin, a blank check to offend God however one wishes as long as one says "Sorry" afterward, and a handy get-out-of-hell-free card.

One must agree that these ideas sell a lot of books; but then, McDonald's sells a lot of "food." Just because millions of people buy something does not make it good for you. A familiar old adage states, "You are what you eat." American Christians have eaten a steady diet of false teaching regarding grace, and we are showing the ill effects in an epidemic of sinful strongholds and spiritual powerlessness.

WHAT'S SO GODLY ABOUT FEAR?

According to Hebrews 12:28-29, one of the functions of God's grace is to inspire in us reverence, awe, and a holy fear of God:

> *Therefore, since we are receiving a kingdom*
> *   which cannot be shaken,*
> *let us have GRACE, by which we may serve*
> *   God acceptably*
> *WITH REVERENCE AND GODLY fear.*
> *   For our God is a consuming fire.*
> Hebrews 12:28-29

"A consuming fire? Isn't that the Old Testament God, before He mellowed during the inter-testamental period? WHAT DO FIRE AND FEAR HAVE TO DO WITH GRACE?" Answer: everything. The modern Church may have reimagined God as a celestial teddy bear, but He remains the same, regardless of our vain imaginations.

According to the New Testament, God is still a holy and consuming fire, and pleasing worship will still contain the elements (among others) of reverence, awe, and holy fear. The fact that we commonly lack such in our worship today further demonstrates that we do not understand nor possess Biblical grace. Lacking true grace leads to falling short of true worship.

JUST REPEAT AFTER ME...

What does it mean to "believe" in Christ, and what impact (if any) should it have on our lives? In an age where the lost are often encouraged to just "accept Christ" or "make a decision" for Him, does Jesus still expect us to surrender our lives, yield our wills, and place His desires ahead of our own?

Jesus set the bar very high for those who would follow Him, while the American Church constantly looks for ways to lower it. When speaking of His followers, Jesus used the term "disciple," one who walked in the footsteps of their Master, and imitated His life and ministry. Christ never required anyone to be His disciple—the choice was always theirs alone. But likewise, never once did Jesus lower the standard of discipleship nor "soft sell" the cost to those who would come after Him. *The cost was the cross.*

> *Then He said to them all,*
> *"If anyone desires to come after Me,*
> *let him deny himself,* ·
> *and take up his cross daily, and follow Me.*
> *For whoever desires to save his life will lose it,*
> *but whoever loses his life for My sake will save it."*
>
> Luke 9:23-24

Note the "If" statement of Jesus! As greatly as He loved the world (*John 3:16*) and recognized His mission "to seek and save the lost" (*Luke 19:10*), Jesus never compromised the standard nor minimized the cost of being His disciple. *Discipleship meant surrendering one's whole life to Christ.* Nothing less was accepted, because anything less would lead to "serving two masters" and thus to destruction.

Christ commissioned us to make disciples that obey His commands (*see Matthew 28:19-20*). Today, we make converts who are unaware that such commands exist. Real evangelism requires making real disciples who are devoted to Jesus, not converts to our way of thinking or brand of religion. However, we tend to reproduce ourselves. If we would **make** disciples, we must first **be** disciples.

Love That Costs Nothing Is Worth Nothing

God's love is often described as "free," which is true in the sense that we have done nothing to deserve it; it is freely given to us. Yet true Christians realize that the full expression of love at the Cross was costly to God beyond all measure. *Real love costs.*

What, then, of our love for Jesus? While the Church has taught that friendship with Jesus is an automatic, instantaneous, and irreversible benefit of saying a sinner's prayer, what does Scripture say about our love for our Savior? Let us consider Jesus' own words from John chapter 14 regarding what He expected to see in the lives of those who would call themselves His friends:

If you love Me, keep My commandments. (v. 15)

He who has My commandments and keeps them, it is he who loves Me. And he who loves Me will be loved by My Father, and I will love him and manifest Myself to him. (v. 21)

Jesus answered and said to him, "If anyone loves Me, he will keep My word… He who does not love Me does not keep My words…" (vv. 23-24)

These verses (and many others) make it clear that *obeying Jesus and loving Jesus are inseparable.* Perhaps one can (for a time) obey Jesus without loving Him, but one cannot love Him without obeying Him. We can sing about being a friend of God on Sunday morning and live void of His friendship on Sunday afternoon if we choose to ignore the vital element of obedience.

I realize that the term "obedience" is not especially popular in the American Church. The very word reminds us of our responsibility to *live our love,* and to follow through on our commitment to Christ. The Church has formed a false dichotomy between "following" Christ and "obeying" Him, as if one can be accomplished without the other. We have told converts that Jesus first becomes their Savior, but later (if they are the extra-spiritual variety) they can make Him Lord.

Hogwash. Christ *is* Lord—in fact, "*KING OF KINGS AND LORD OF LORDS*" *(Revelation 19:16)*—whether or not we embrace Him as such in our personal lives. He is not running a campaign to be elected the next "lord of our lives." Since He alone died for us, He accepts no competitors for the Lordship and authority of His Church. And the Church will never know a return to spiritual power and influence without utter submission to His authority and wholehearted obedience to His commands. If we believe otherwise, we are woefully deceived.

HIS COMMANDMENTS ARE NOT BURDENSOME

All honest Christians realize that they "fall short of the glory of God." God is perfect; you and I are not. Embracing the truth of our responsibility to obey Jesus does not mean taking on a heavy burden, nor adhering to a legalistic system of works. *Obedience is about relationship,* not mere religion. It is a loving response to the Savior, not a legalistic effort to earn His favor.

Scripture is clear that none of us obey God perfectly (see 1 John 1:8-10 if you are in doubt). However, God desires that His children possess a wholehearted love for Him. And one of the natural fruits of that love, like thankfulness and worship, will be obeying His Word and His will, pressing "toward the goal for the prize of the upward call of God in Christ Jesus" *(Philippians 3:14).* A churchgoer with no desire to obey Christ's Word and possessing no remorse over their sin must face the sobering reality that 1) they are not a friend of God, and 2) they have strayed from their First Love, or 3) that they never knew Him in the first place.

A Word to My Fellow Pastors

Multitudes in the American Church do not know Jesus, and most do not know that they do not know. Pastors, it is time for us to first *LIVE* our love for Jesus so passionately that the people will see it, and then *PREACH* our love for Jesus so boldly that they will hear it. *We must become the message we are trying to proclaim*—a message of God's love that forgives, of His power that conquers sin, and of His Spirit that transforms a life.

Recent surveys indicate that the average American pastor is spending about 30 minutes weekly in personal time with God in prayer, worship, and Bible study. Pastors, *we are impoverished beyond belief,* and thus are feeding only husks to God's flock. If we do not see the fire of God fall on the pulpit, how can we ask for it to fall on the pew? If we do not tend the holy flame of our own First Love, how can we counsel others to do better?

America is in the direst need of revival. It is time for pastors to stir themselves up to seek God at any cost. Turn off the TV. Cancel your internet service. Take steps that offend the flesh and may even appear radical, and *set aside daily time to seek the face of God.* Return to your First Love, and God will return with power to your life, marriage, family, and ministry. He will be found by us when we seek Him with all our hearts. The time is short, my brothers; let us pursue the Lord.

CHAPTER 8

Warning:
An Emergent-C in the Church

EVERY CULTURE HAS ITS FADS, and the church culture is no exception. To be successful, any fad must capture the attention of the masses—especially of the younger generation—by offering an idea or style that looks novel (like something new under the sun), thus urging them to follow with enthusiasm. This is exactly what the "emergent" movement is doing in the American Church.

Many chapters could be devoted to the origins of the "emergent movement," and to the philosophy and considerable doctrinal errors of its leaders. For those interested in further reading on this topic, Roger Oakland's book *Faith Undone* amply addresses the subject.

In this chapter, we will examine several observations that should prove challenging and helpful to those of an emergent persuasion. These are shared out of love for brothers and sisters who are drawn to the emergent church as a cultural expression, but who may not have considered some of its potential pitfalls:

- **A Culture of Compromise:** Emergent church teaching and practice commonly shows a willingness to *minimize and compromise Biblical truth* for the sake of appearing "relevant" to the secular world. This is a fatal flaw, one that makes this "movement" ripe for heresy, and for leading young Christians to disaster.
- **Imitating the World:** Although claiming to be relevant to postmodern culture, the emergent movement often smacks insincere and hollow to the lost because it is *imitative instead of creative*. It simply follows the world on areas like how to dress, what music to listen to, what movies to watch, who to vote for, and how to feel about social and cultural issues. The fruit of following the world's lead is inevitably compromise, for "the whole world lies under the sway of the wicked one" *(1 John 5:19)*. The counsel of Scripture is dangerously missing from the emergent world view.

The reasoning behind such imitation of the world says, *"If we act and dress more like the world, we will have a more relevant witness to them."* The intended result (in theory) is that the lost will be drawn by our externalities—clothing and hair, tattoos and piercings, liberal social agendas and compromised standards—and will thus join the church. This thinking assumes that the lost are inherently shallow, and that we will reach them by being the same. And when we do make a convert, we unknowingly set them on a course of shallow, me-centered Christianity, as this is what we have modeled for them.

In reality, the "evangelize our culture by compromising with them" approach has been tried repeatedly in previous generations (Spurgeon wrote about it in the 1800's), and always with the same results: it does not work, because it is not Biblical. Dr. Tozer put it this way: *"Modern Christians hope to save the world by being like it, but it will never work. The Church's power over the world springs out of her unlikeness to it, never from her integration into it."*

66

WHAT TRUE RELEVANCE LOOKS LIKE

In the late 1950's, a young preacher named David Wilkerson stumbled out of rural Pennsylvania and onto the streets of New York City to share the love of Christ with members of a ruthless inner-city gang. But by emergent standards, he did it all wrong: he failed to look and act the part of an Hispanic gang member. He did not use foul street language. He wore no gang garb, and did not carry a knife. He simply went into those murderous, drug-infested slums with nothing but the love of Christ, the Word of God, and the leading and power of the Holy Spirit. The result of his obedience was miraculous salvations, changed lives, drug addicts set free by the power of the Holy Spirit, and a move of God so powerful that it has touched countless thousands of lives all over the world through Teen Challenge, the ministry that was birthed at that time. (Every Christian should read *The Cross and the Switchblade*, which chronicles Reverend Wilkerson's story. It is a modern classic, and will edify your faith tremendously).

Wilkerson's example underscores the truth that *it is not the "outside of the cup" that matters, but rather, what is on the inside.* The presence of God's Spirit, a life of genuine love, a humble and worshipful heart—these are the precious commodities in a disciple's life that will draw the lost to the Savior. And developing such fruit takes time, focus, dedication, and surrender to the Lord's will and ways. It is not as simple as getting a tattoo or a new hairstyle. *The things that really count for Jesus require sacrifice on our parts, and there is no substitute.*

But has God ever called someone to dress like the people group they are trying to reach for Christ? Certainly He has, as the life and ministry of J. Hudson Taylor vividly illustrate. Taylor went to China as a missionary in the 1850's, and adopted the dress and culture of a Chinese peasant. His ministry bore incredible fruit: he personally led thousands to Christ, founded the China Inland Mission by which many other missionaries were sent to the field, and is considered the father of modern missions. For

Taylor, adopting the cultural expression of the people to whom he was sent was a vital part of effectively presenting the Gospel.

However, Hudson Taylor demonstrated some qualities that the emergent movement typically does not. He 1) was led by the Spirit, 2) was empowered by the Spirit, 3) presented the true Gospel, 4) sought to exalt Christ in all he did, 5) was willing to endure great suffering for the sake of the Gospel, and 6) made true disciples that loved and obeyed God's Word, making no attempt to mimic worldly ways. Today's obsession with "relevance" among many in the American Church (and especially amongst emergent leaders) falls far short of the goal, methodology, and fruit displayed in Taylor's life.

SPIRITUAL DEPTH... WHAT A CONCEPT

This may sound archaic, but there is nothing so relevant as the pure presentation of the Gospel of Christ. Even in our postmodern, 21st century culture, people are desperately needy for genuine love. They do not need us to look or act like them in our dress and speech. They need us to love God with all our heart, soul, mind, and strength, and to love our neighbor as ourself. If we will return to our Biblical calling, we will be *genuinely* relevant to this world again.

Ultimately, the world needs us to be a humble and holy people *(Zephaniah 3:12)*, wholehearted in our devotion to Jesus, and with lives set apart for the Savior. Although "holiness" is not a word often mentioned by emergent leaders, any church or Christian who believes that one can have a powerful witness to the world without pursuing God's holiness is simply deceived. "Pursue peace with all people, and **holiness, without which no one will see the Lord**" *(Hebrews 12:14)*. This is diametrically opposed to the mindset of compromise that is so common today. While compromise may produce some short-term numerical success—much like the seed planted in shallow, rocky soil that Jesus described in Matthew

13:5—there will be no true disciples made. Remember, the plant grew up quickly, but died the same, for *it lacked depth of soil.*

- **Ministering from a Shallow Experience of Christ** *(and teaching others to do the same).* Lack of depth is a hallmark of the emergent movement. All too often, emergent leaders are men inexperienced in God's Word and lacking the depth and maturity that comes from walking the path of discipleship with Christ. Many would appear to know little of the cost of following Christ, of being crucified with Him, of laying down one's life to serve the Church, and of living for the glory of the Savior. Instead, a great deal of focus is placed on appearance, for image is everything in the emergent movement—appearance over substance, sound bites over sound doctrine. A wise old saying states, *"Only follow the guide who's been where you want to go."* Judging by their books and teachings, many emergent leaders cannot lead young Believers into the deeper life of fellowship with Christ because they have not gone there themselves.
- **Rejecting Yesterday's Powerless Religion; Creating Tomorrow's Powerless Religion.** Emergent Christianity has attempted to define itself by what it is *not*—that it is *not* like the stuffy, religious, uncool church experience of the previous generation. This is accomplished by shaking off the religious formalities and external trappings of traditional church, and by creating a cultural expression that is theoretically more relevant to young people (and to certain middle-aged people who are still clinging to illusions of being young). In reality, however, the emergent movement *merely replaces one set of man-made externalities and cultural norms with another.* In the process, emergent churches avoid the letter of the law by embracing lawlessness, and avoid the sin of legalism by embracing compromise.

This may be nothing more than misguided zeal, but it is potentially disastrous for those who are led to believe that this equates to Biblical Christianity. And the sad irony of the emergent movement is that while supposing to break from the dead formalities and powerless religion of the past, its leaders are actually managing to steer the ship *farther from the power and presence of* God than even their religious forefathers. They are creating a church whose greatest concern is not the glory of God, but the opinions and approval of man. At best it will be impotent; at worst, it is *ichabod—the glory has departed from His house.*

- **It is a Mutt.** Some of the most influential emergent church leaders claim to be "reimagining" or reshaping Christianity, both in form and in theology, to be more applicable to the culture of our day. However, the fruit of their imagination is "Christian" in name only, not in theology or fruit. In reality, it is a doctrinal mutt, an undesirable mixture of various streams of religious influence and practice including Catholicism, Eastern religions, and New Age. Both in practice and doctrine, emergent churches are narrowing the gap between the Church and the world, and slouching toward the one-world religion of the antichrist.

- **"It's All About Me, Really..."** Lastly, emergent teaching idolizes **personal expression** as the measure and goal of Christian experience. Listen to the conversation of some young emergent Christians, and you may find that a frequent theme of discourse is "What's acceptable with God?" (In other words, "How far can I go without *really* sinning?") This is commonly reflected in the teachings and the examples of emergent leaders. They teach that God is so into relationship, so into *you,* that He cares little about behavior and the archaic concepts of holiness and obedience. Thanks to our "liberty in Christ," emergent followers are taught that God is definitely OK with alcohol, smoking, foul language, and the dress and entertainment of the world. And He *might* be OK with premarital sex and homosexuality (depending on which emergent leader's book you are reading).

Needless to say, the latter of those statements is unbridled heresy. However, even when considering the previous statements, one is inclined to ask, "What does expressing 'Christian liberty' in the form of beer, cigars, profanity, and worldly entertainment have to do with growth in Christ?"

"All things are lawful for me," the apostle stated when addressing the Believers in Corinth, "but not all things are profitable." The question for a disciple of Christ is never, *"Can I?"* but rather, *"Should I? How will this bring glory to Christ, build up His Church, and draw the lost to Jesus?"*

A true Christian is one who has been bought with Jesus' blood. Their body is a temple of the Holy Spirit, and "their" life is no longer their own to do with as they choose *(1 Corinthians 6:19-20)*. Christians are commissioned to bring God glory in everything, large or small—even what we "eat or drink" *(1 Corinthians 10:31)*. Any expression of "Christian liberty" which draws attention to my*self* rather than my *Savior* is falling short of my calling, and will be at the expense of others. Christ sets us at liberty to seek the glory of the King, the good of the Church, and the salvation of the lost. Much of what the American Church deems "liberty" is, in reality, license for sin.

REIMAGINE THIS...

Let us suppose for a moment that God has given a big, postmodern, 21st century green light to all forms of self-expression. We Christians are hereby invited (even encouraged) to express ourselves with tattoos and piercings, holding a smoldering stogie in one hand and a Coors in the other, while our iPod cranks out some vintage Rolling Stones. Now we are liberated, free from our parents' stuffy church culture and empowered to be just as cool as we know how. We can hang out in bars, watch R-rated movies, learn some four-letter words, sport low-cut dresses, get a fake tan, pierce our eyebrows—why, we can do most *anything we want* because we are no longer following the cultural norms of the American Church. FREEDOM!!!

The question looms large in the thinking person's mind: *so what?* Do we really believe that the world is impressed? That we have advanced the Kingdom of God? That souls will rise up on that Day to say, "I never would have come to know Jesus if you hadn't dressed so cool... smoked... cussed... hung out in that bar on Hawthorne Street... thank you! Thank you!"

EXPRESS SELF, OR DENY SELF

Self-expression may be the way of the world, but it will never be the way of the Kingdom. It is (by definition) tied to "self," and self must die, for Christ made the standard of discipleship "deny yourself." We will never bear good fruit for Christ, never build His Church, never draw the lost to the Savior, and never touch the hurting with His love so long as we are bound to the tyranny of self.

Christ did not call us to coolness, but to a cross. Many adherents of this movement would do well to lay down their copy of the newest "reinvent what the Bible says" emergent book, and pick up the Bible itself; to take their eyes off of the latest "cool guy with ADHD teaching New Age but calling it Christianity" DVD, and fix their eyes on Jesus; to lay down their self-expression, and take up their cross.

Dietrich Bonhoeffer said, "When Christ calls a man, He bids him come and die." That is the challenge to every person reading this book: the life you seek will never be found by seeking life, but only by seeking to bring glory to Christ. *As you live for the King of Glory, your life will reflect the glory of the King.*

Lose yourself in the pursuit of your Savior, and live with reckless abandon after His Presence. "Count all things loss" that you may gain Christ. You will discover what the great saints have always found to be true without exception: the Presence of Christ is more than enough. It is an "exceedingly great reward," and His presence is fullness of joy.

CHAPTER 9

Of Shepherds and Kings

THE CHURCH TODAY CAN LEARN MUCH from young King Rehoboam. In 1 Kings 12:1-16, we see the newly-crowned king with an important decision before him: what sort of monarch was he going to be? His father Solomon had been a popular and wise ruler in his younger years, but as he hardened his heart to the LORD, it inevitably affected his heart for the people entrusted to his leadership. Now Rehoboam must decide if he would walk in the errors of his father, or follow in the footsteps of his grandfather David.

Rehoboam solicited the counsel of two sets of advisors. First came the advice of the elders who had served his father Solomon and had seen the consequences of his sin. They spoke thus: "If you will *BE A SERVANT to these people today, and SERVE THEM, and answer them, and speak good words to them,* then they will be your servants forever" *(1 Kings 12:7).* These wise men were advocating for Rehoboam to embrace servant-leadership and to learn to become a shepherd over the people of God as King David had done:

*So he shepherded them according
to the integrity of his heart,
And guided them by the skillfulness of his hands.*

Psalm 78:72

Rehoboam rejected this counsel, choosing instead to heed the advice of his contemporaries, the young men with whom he had grown up. Their counsel was essentially to beat the people into submission, demand forced servitude, and to lead through intimidation. It was terrible advice and led to the ultimate schism: the dividing of Israel into the northern and southern kingdoms. And it was the first of many tragic mistakes by a young king who had a high regard for himself, but had little regard for the people he was called to lead.

SOUND FAMILIAR?

The American Church has more than a little "Rehoboam" about her. Like Solomon's son, pastors today are presented with a call to shepherd God's people and to model sacrificial and servant-hearted leadership. And much like Rehoboam, church leaders often choose instead to emulate the leadership style of the world, perceived as wise contemporaries.

Let us consider but a few examples of how this error manifests in our day. Seeker-sensitive churches have long been enamored with corporate leadership philosophies, even though they run at odds with Jesus' teaching and example. "Successful Leader" conferences (that strongly resemble a Tony Robbins seminar) draw professional ministers like moths to a flame, teaching formulas to "grow your church" and "increase your income." "Anything that's healthy will grow," we pastors are told. Perhaps…but then, mold grows pretty well in the right setting. If gaining adherents is the surest sign of health, then Marxism was the healthiest ideology of the mid-20th century.

Since we have lost the art of discerning spiritual fruit, we measure growth by bucks in the budget and pulses in the pews. Numbers up? Good growth! Numbers down? Time to go to another church growth seminar!

But the error is not only found in the market-driven megachurch. Traditional churches are also not exempt from Rehoboam's style of leadership. Countless churches have become entrenched in political battles between boards and committees, elders and deacons, pastors and parishioners, as individuals and ministries fight for their fair share of the church turf and budget (in the name of Christ). Personality conflicts have led to church coups, schisms, splits, and hostile takeovers, as egos collide between the temple porch and the altar. Many a church, dividing over "doctrinal differences," has in reality been nothing more than stubborn human pride unwilling to admit error and to repent. Our lack of making mature disciples shows its full fruit in the realm of church leadership.

But the clearest example of the Rehoboam dilemma is in the pulpits of our churches. This, I believe, is the greatest earthly lack in the American Church. We have pulpits, we have personalities, we have preachers, but we have precious few *pastors*.

WANTED: SHEPHERDS

What is a "pastor?" Today, we often think of a pastor as "someone who fills a pulpit on Sunday morning." However, the New Testament gives a remarkably clear definition of what a pastor truly is: a shepherd, one who cares for the sheep, nurturing and feeding them, leading and defending them (with his life, if need be). In fact, the Greek word used for "pastor" in Ephesians 4:11 is the same word used in Jesus' statement, "he who enters by the door is the *shepherd* of the sheep" *(John 10:2)*. *Pastors are called to serve God's sheep, feed God's flock, and be utterly devoted to their nurture, growth, and care.*

Today's minister may be expected to have many gifts. Perhaps he is a dynamic orator, a gifted evangelist, or a shrewd administrator. In reality, he may possess all these skills and more, but *if he does not have God's heart to nurture, lead, and feed God's people, he is not a shepherd.* Our lack of true shepherds in the American Church is largely to blame for our spiritual malnourishment. We have many professional ministers, but few pastors; many kings, but few shepherds.

IT'S A CALLING, NOT A CAREER

Today the path to the pulpit in evangelical churches typically takes a young man through some sort of Bible school, perhaps onto seminary, and then arriving at the prized possession: a diploma! Having memorized information, completed courses, taken tests, and done all the ministry training program required, he has finally graduated. Now, a special term ("licensing," or "credentials," or "ordination" depending on the denomination) is bestowed upon the young man, and he is thereby pronounced *a pastor.* He may now kiss the bride.

From this point he will begin to apply for church jobs, probably starting with a smaller assignment, and (he hopes) working his way up the clerical ladder to a bigger church with more people in a nicer part of town. While there are certainly other roads to the "throne," this process is normative.

What is wrong with this picture? Primarily this: we have made becoming a pastor no different than becoming an electrician or beautician or science teacher. We have lost the realization that *man does not call pastors—God does.* Caring for God's people is a high and holy calling requiring a sacred anointing and sanctified life. It is the most cherished trust on earth, for it is nurturing the Body of Christ, helping prepare the Bride for the return of her Groom. This is not something one decides he wants to do; it must be a calling from the Most High.

Spurgeon wrote, *"May we never venture upon hallowed exercises without sacred anointings."* This was written to describe *every* Christian's work and worship for the Lord. How much more should it be said for those who would lead and feed God's flock?

As a youth, I once asked a staff pastor at a large denominational church how he got into ministry work. Something about his reply deeply troubled me, and I have never forgotten his words: "Well, many years ago I knew that I was called to be a professional golfer. But I missed my calling, and the opportunity escaped me. So I asked myself, 'What should I do now?' I knew I could *always* get into the ministry, so that's the direction I went."

When in doubt, use shepherding God's people as a safety net, a handy "plan B" when one has missed their true calling. Many a professional minister could confess similar reasoning that led to their present role, although few would be so honest about it. Not a few ministers have set their primary goal as retirement and enjoying their denomination's pension package. For others, their goal is to work their way up the denominational ladder so they can get out of the local church scene and into the hierarchal church government. This is not to suggest that pensions or promotions are inherently evil, but they are no motivation for someone to serve as a shepherd.

One Term Fits All?

According to Ephesians chapter 4, God gave the Church apostles, prophets, evangelists, teachers, and pastors—unique roles for unique God-given gifts and callings. For the most part, in today's Church we have just one role: pastor. Whatever your gift and calling, if you want to minister, we call you a pastor. But if God does not call you a pastor, then both you and the churches where you serve will suffer the needless consequences of having the right man in the wrong job.

There are many examples of this pattern in churches today. Perhaps most common is the scenario where the local church "pastor" is actually an "evangelist," one gifted and appointed by God to get people saved. Since we do not typically hire evangelists in the American Church, countless evangelists are attempting to serve as shepherds. While some evangelists can learn to pastor by gaining God's heart for the flock, others find frustration in a pastoral role, for they were never designed to be tending the flock, but rather searching for lost sheep.

As such, their preaching may tend to be long on conviction, but short on comfort; long on altar calls, but shy on using God's Word to teach the people how to love and obey Him. This may seem like good evangelism, but a steady diet of such preaching will make for some hungry sheep, because it fails to truly feed the flock and train them to be disciples. Having the right men in the wrong job has proved detrimental to the health of the Church, and has hamstrung our effectiveness in advancing God's Kingdom.

LISTENING TO OUR ELDERS

There is another way in which we tend to resemble Rehoboam in the American Church. Like the young king, we choose to listen to the popular voices of our day rather than choosing the wisdom of those who have gone before us. Primarily, this relates to our negligence in teaching God's Word, and in failing to heed and obey its counsel in how we are to live (both individually and as churches).

But secondarily, this applies to the host of contemporary voices whose books and teachings attempt to guide today's Christian through the journey they call "self-discovery." Evangelical Christendom is flooded with popular books and programs, yet the floodwaters are wide but shallow. Undoubtedly, there are many well-meaning Christians involved in this enterprise.

And just as certainly, there are many fortunes being made by the merchandising of God's people. Whatever the motivation of the authors, publishers, and distributors of all this needless paraphernalia, the result is clear: the American Church gleans her counsel from her contemporaries, and drinks from waters that are muddied with the world's ideas and values.

This is not to suggest that all books being written and published by Christians today are without spiritual truth or benefit. However, an honest assessment quickly reveals that the most popular books typically contain the least meat (and sometimes the most subtly-placed heresy). Go to your local Christian bookstore and you will find much "cotton candy" on the shelves. These books offer little substance and even less lasting value because they are shallow in God's Word and long on the ideas of man. Long on sugar, short on meat. Meanwhile, God's flock suffers from an advanced case of spiritual malnourishment while being progressively poisoned by the ways of the world in Christ's Name.

VOICES FROM THE PAST

Thankfully, we have other wells from which we may draw waters of encouragement. Countless followers of Jesus have been richly blessed by the writings of great saints who have gone before us, men like Charles Spurgeon, Oswald Chambers, A.W. Tozer, A.B. Simpson, Andrew Murray, E.M. Bounds, and Leonard Ravenhill, to name but a few. Their lives and their writings have stood the test of time, and offer the Believer genuine encouragement and real meat to help in our walk with Christ.

Any serious disciple of Christ should consider doing two things that will prove a tremendous blessing to your faith (these are purely supplementary to your daily time in God's Word, prayer, and worship). First, use one of the great devotional books as a part of your daily time with the Lord (*My Utmost for His*

Highest by Chambers and *Morning and Evening* by Spurgeon are among the best). Second, read the biographies of some of the great men and women of God. The lives of people like George Mueller, Amy Carmichael, Robert Murray McCheyne, D. L. Moody, Charles Finney, J. Hudson Taylor, and others will encourage your faith and increase your vision for what God can do with one life wholly yielded to Him. Warren Wiersbe has written some excellent books that chronicle the lives of many of these saints, and will help the reader get acquainted with some of the spiritual giants of God's Kingdom.

TIME TO FEED THE FLOCK

For the American Church to return to her calling, there must be a restoration of true shepherds to the Body of Christ. We will never be equipped to make disciples unless we have men appointed and anointed by God to feed and lead the flock. But raising up true shepherds will require much prayer and commitment on the part of the Church, and none of it is possible apart from the help and power of God.

Let us prayerfully consider these imperatives:

1. We pastors must examine ourselves in the light of God's Word and Spirit, making sure that we are called and anointed by Him to be a shepherd. The appointment of man does not necessarily equal the calling of God.
2. Pastors must make our **FIRST LOVE** our first priority. **Unless we are actively pursuing deeper fellowship with Christ in our daily lives, we have no business attempting to lead the Church.**

   Amy Carmichael, a woman mightily used by God on the mission field in India, wrote that *"the work will never go deeper than we have gone ourselves."* Far too many pastors go only as deep as deemed necessary to keep the wheels of ministry turning. Bible study is reduced to "getting the theme for my next sermon series," prayer is belittled to "asking God's blessing on my ministry," and worship only happens during church services. The inevitable result is a starved spiritual life and broken fellowship with God. The living waters of which Jesus spoke cease to flow through us, and we minister out of a self-made cistern of human effort.

Oswald Chambers preached, *"The measure of the worth of our public activity for God is the private profound communion we have with Him. Rush is wrong every time, there is always plenty of time to worship God."* We pastors would do well to refrain from public preaching until our private communion is full and flowing once again. Let us cease giving the flock stale bread and regurgitated truths. If we seek to love Him with all our heart, soul, mind and strength, God *will* visit our churches (and preaching) with His power. And the fresh "manna" we bring from our revitalized relationship with Christ may prove potent in reviving the flock's appetite for the meat of God's Word.

3. Many true shepherds have strayed from the Biblical role of feeding and leading God's people. If that is true of us, we must set aside the distractions and diversions we have allowed to sway us, resolutely refusing to be caught in the hectic pace of modern ministry any longer, and return to our calling to serve the flock God has entrusted to our care. A wise old saint once said, *"Beware the barrenness of a busy life."* It could well be added: beware the barrenness of a church where the pastor is too busy to shepherd the flock. We must return to God's priorities for pastors, for the health of the Body of Christ.

4. Pastors must wholeheartedly abandon the rampant ministerial pride which is afflicting the American Church

today, choosing instead to bring glory to the One who alone is worthy.

The severity of this problem in our churches today cannot be overstated. If vain glory and personal kingdom building were water, the American Church would be flooded, and the whole nation would be dampened with the overflow of our pride. Competition, self-seeking, pursuing numbers and worldly ideas of "success"—these have taken a devastating toll on the Church. We must repent of every way we have shared in these sins, and we must return to God's Word and ways. Let us remember Charles E. Jefferson's admonition to preachers: *"A shepherd cannot shine... His work calls for continuous self-effacement... Every good shepherd lays down his life for the sheep."* If we will heed this counsel, God will be magnified in our lives and ministries, and the impact on the Church (and our nation) will be glorious.

5. Some have made ministry a means of pursuing material gain, and as a result have been guilty of "fleecing the flock" instead of feeding them. If that be the case with us, we must repent before God and before the church that has witnessed our poor example. We must remember that our reward was never intended to be earthly, and that one day soon we will stand before the Throne of God and answer for the way we cared for His people. Let us put away all greed and every tendency to feed our flesh, and diligently seek God to restore to us a heart of humility and servanthood.

6. Many pastors have ignored Jesus' call to servant-leadership, choosing instead to use coercion, guilt, manipulation, and a heavy-handed style of leadership—and all of it done in Jesus' Name. The tragic effects of this trend are beyond words, but the partial fruit can be seen in the disenfranchised masses who love Christ but fear

the church. May each of us who serve as pastors lay our hearts bare before the Lord, asking Him to show us the ways in which we have "lorded it over" His people rather than having served them with love and patience *(Matthew 20:25).* If we humble our hearts, He will be faithful to convict and cleanse us, and to show us a path of repentance and humility before those whom we have injured with our sin.

7. Lastly, some will realize they are the "right man in the wrong job," operating in a role to which God never called or appointed them. These must first surrender to God's will and ways, being willing to do anything and everything God indicates. Then, they must seek wise counsel from God's Word and Spirit, and likely from other trustworthy leaders who can give perspective and Godly advice on how to best address and heal the situation. The result will be greater health and fruitfulness, both in the local church and in the life and ministry of the minister.

These are difficult steps, ones which require humility, brokenness, a yielded will, and much grace from God. However, they are absolutely vital, utterly indispensable. If we are serious about participating in the return of the American Church to her God-ordained influence and authority, then we must see the restoration of true shepherds. All American Christians must ask God to raise up shepherds after His own heart to lead His Church again. We will never be fit for revival until His House is set in order.

And I will give you shepherds according to My heart, who will feed you with knowledge and understanding.

Jeremiah 3:15

CHAPTER 10

God's Plan for a Glorious Church

*That He might present her to Himself
    a glorious church,
not having spot or wrinkle or any such thing,
but that she should be holy and without blemish.*

Ephesians 5:27

GOD HAS ORDAINED THAT HE WILL RETURN for a glorious Church, a people of praise, pure speech, and pleasing worship *(see Zephaniah 3:9-13)*. They are a victorious Church that is unflinching in the face of sacrifice, suffering, or even death so long as it means glory for their King:

*And they overcame him by the blood of the Lamb
and by the word of their testimony,
and they did not love their lives to the death.*

Revelation 12:11

That description does not much resemble the American Church of our day, does it? In fact, American Christianity today is so far from the Biblical norm that *one is tempted to wonder if there is any possible reconciling of the two.* Truly, only a God as great as ours could have a plan to take this sleeping giant and awaken a vibrant, anointed, loving, uncompromising, glorious Church. But how will He do it? I believe the answer is a simple one: suffering.

"Not so!" I hear some protesting. "Suffering is for Christians in places like China, not a *Christian* nation like ourselves."

Suffering, especially suffering for our faith, is a concept unwelcome and largely foreign to the contemporary American Church. This is because we have been influenced and even defined by the culture around us, and our culture is one of rampant self-interest. At all costs, Americans have sought personal gain and comfort over corporate good or national well-being, and the devastating results are on the front page of our newspapers every day.

But nowhere are the tragic effects of the "self at any price" culture more visible than in the Church. We are the one institution on the face of the earth *designed, called,* and *expected* to be decidedly **NOT** about "self," but entirely "other"—living for the glory of God, for the good of His Church, and for the saving of lost souls. And if we will reclaim that high and holy calling, we will find ourselves **empowered** once more to fulfill our mission.

Preaching about "sacrifice" is quite unpopular these days, and it is unlikely that one can build a megachurch or become a Christian celebrity with such a message. However, the reality of the last days is starting to set in upon us, and the storm is about to hit our nation in a big, bad way. Multitudes who have clung to empty promises of personal fulfillment offered by their favorite televangelists will be shaken to their core.

Countless churchgoers who have believed that Christ's call was to *"self-discovery"* instead of *self-sacrifice* will find themselves adrift on stormy seas of adversity, lacking the anchor of a vital knowledge and experience of God's Word. Our shallow, me-centered theology will wear thin in the reality of lack, persecution, and suffering.

In such a day, people will start to seek a *real* faith in a *real* Savior who can provide *real* hope and help. And those who really know God—who have proved His promises and tasted His goodness, who have been through battles and seen His faithfulness—such people will be magnets for the hurting and questioning ones. Then the Word of God in our hearts and on our lips will be a healing balm to wounded souls, a beacon of salvation pointing the lost to the Savior.

This generation of Christians has been given milk (or perhaps formula), but the day calls for meat. They have been coddled like little children, when the battle needs men. Never have so many churches and denominations possessed so little real spiritual power. Never have so many worn the title "Christian" with so little understanding of what the term denotes, and so little resemblance of the One whose name we bear. And never has the need been greater for a true awakening among God's people, a shattering of our slumber and a shaking of our idolatry.

There is yet time. We serve a gracious God who hears our prayers, tests our hearts, and will "show Himself strong on behalf of those whose heart is loyal to Him" *(2 Chronicles 16:9)*. But *the hour is late and the need is urgent.* Failure to heed and obey the call of God at this crucial point of history will prove disastrous for the Church and for America. It is time for God's people to *press in,* to pursue His presence with passionate prayer, to lay hold of His throne of grace and cry out for His mercy which "triumphs over judgment" *(James 2:13).*

RETURNING THROUGH PRAYER

Souls hang in the balance, and eternal destinies are being decided. Will you enlist your heart and prayers to share the burden of the Savior for a dying world? Will you set aside your personal gains and goals to pursue the agenda and plans of the Most High?

God's aviary has numerous turkeys and countless chickens, but God is looking for a few eagles, men and women whom He can trust with His power and purposes. God is seeking for a people whose hearts are set after the Savior, who love Jesus more than life itself, and who would rather die than deny or defame the One who saved their souls. The call is extended to each of us, for God is no respecter of persons. Every follower of Christ must decide how he or she will respond to the Savior.

Count the cost soberly, and choose wisely; for the weight of this decision will have eternal impact, both for your life and for others.

CHAPTER 11

Satan's Agenda for Our Nation

THERE IS A GREAT SPIRITUAL BATTLE being waged for our nation. The soul of this country is at stake, and Satan's agenda is one of lawlessness, where good is called bad, and right is called wrong. What Scripture calls "wickedness" is first tolerated, then celebrated, then sanctioned and protected by law. Intact family units become the exception, a culture of death is promoted, the vilest forms of entertainment become mainstream, the media holds the greatest sway over public opinion, our pitiful public education system continues to produce young people who cannot think for themselves, and those who hold Biblical ideas regarding right and wrong are dismissed and shouted down as hate mongers. Add a Wall Street meltdown, persistent joblessness, and protracted economic upheaval and you have a perfect setup for a once-great nation to embrace socialism at the very least, perhaps much worse.

How did we arrive at such a point? What doors were opened that allowed Satan's kingdom to have such influence and sway over the hearts and minds of so many Americans?

SATAN'S AGENDA FOR THE CHURCH

To understand what is taking place in our nation, we must start at the Church. The painful reality is that *the responsibility for America's sad moral state falls squarely on the shoulders of the American Church.* Our nation has only become what we have allowed due to our spiritual sloth, complacency, compromise and even rebellion.

There is mischief afoot in the Church. Both through what we have taught and what we have *failed* to teach, we have allowed Satan's agenda to take root in the world view of American Christianity. Harry Blamires wrote regarding the Church in the early 1960's, *"We have lost the Christian mind,"* that is, the ability to work out the mind of Christ *(1 Corinthians 2:16b)* as it applies to moral and cultural issues of our day.

Over 40 years later, the Church has simply lost her mind. We have lost the ability to think clearly on matters of doctrine, lost the awareness of our desperate spiritual state, and lost the sense of the impending judgment coming to our nation unless there is a massive spiritual awakening. Many Christians today are more concerned about the numbers in their 401K than about the number of souls passing to eternal banishment in the lake of fire. We have adopted an *excessively temporal mindset,* where we are so earthly-minded that we are of no heavenly good. Decades of man-centered, me-first Christianity have taken a dreadful toll on the spiritual life of the Church. And we are reaping the bitter fruit in our nation and society.

The good news is this: the challenges and trials of the days ahead give the American Church our greatest opportunity to wake up, see our need, and begin seeking God's face again. Consider the words of the late Stephen Olford:

"It is my conviction that we are never going to have revival until God has brought the church of Jesus Christ to the point of desperation. As long as

Christian people can trust religious organization, material wealth, popular preaching, shallow evangelistic crusades and promotion drives, there will never be revival. *BUT WHEN CONFIDENCE IN THE FLESH IS SMASHED*, and the church comes to the realization of her desperate wretchedness, blindness and nakedness before God, *THEN AND ONLY THEN WILL GOD BREAK IN*."

RECLAIMING THE CHURCH

Can America be saved, or are we on an irreversible course toward the moral abyss and the trash heap of history? **The answer lies with the Church.** If America is to be reclaimed for truth, justice, and good, then the Church must first be reclaimed for her King. This battle must be fought and won in the hearts and minds of God's people, one life and one prayer at a time, because revivals always start with a persevering minority who become mighty in prayer. God needs no "majority rule" (remember Gideon's victorious 300). God shook the most powerful nation on earth through one shepherd named Moses, turned the moral tide in apostate Israel through one prophet named Elijah, and confounded all the schemes of Satan and his demonic minions through the Son of Man, Jesus Christ. In times since, God has rocked the world and shaken the heavenlies when He found one man who would wholly believe Him, men like Wycliffe, Luther, Whitefield, Wesley, and Finney. There is no end to what God can do through even one who will believe and pray. The Scriptural call is as clear for us today as it was in the prophet Hosea's time:

> *Come, and LET US RETURN TO THE LORD;*
> *For He has torn, but He will heal us;*
> *He has stricken, but He will bind us up…*
> *LET US PURSUE the knowledge of the LORD.*

His going forth is established as the morning;
HE WILL COME TO US LIKE THE RAIN,
Like the latter and former rain to the earth.

Hosea 6:1,3

THE BATTLE LINES ARE DRAWN

To wage effective prayer-warfare on behalf of the Church, we need to clearly see where the battle lines are drawn and the nature of the deception coming against the Body of Christ in this late hour of history. Here is an overview of some of the specific points in Satan's agenda of deception and compromise for the American Church:

Abandoning the trustworthiness of the Bible. An increasing number of churchgoers no longer believe in the absolute trustworthiness and literal truth of God's Word. The impact of this cannot be overstated, for if you compromise the Word, you have compromised all else. Either God's Word is entirely reliable and applicable, or it is entirely up to the individual to pick and choose as he sees fit. Moreover, without God's inspired and infallible Word, Christianity becomes just another world religion, merely one of the "many paths up the same mountain" to God. If we do not believe in a God who is great enough to preserve the truth and integrity of His Word through the centuries, then we have a larger problem.

Abandoning the belief of hell. The idea of a teddy bear God who is too nice to send anyone to hell will gain increased acceptance in the years ahead within the Church.

Increasing acceptance of the following:

- **Divorce.** Current divorce rates in the Church run parallel to those in the world.
- **Immodesty in dress.** Our love for the world inevitably comes out in what we wear (or fail to wear), and those

who express concern are quickly labeled judgmental, old-fashioned, and the dreaded "irrelevant."

- **Premarital sex.** Young adult churchgoers in particular are following our culture's trend toward seeing premarital sex as "OK." Although many have grown up in churches, their education has come more from television than from Scripture.

- **Homosexuality.** This will be one of the most divisive issues in the next decade within the Church. The Church has been caricatured (both by the media and by those advancing the radical homosexual agenda) as being a group of angry, stone-throwing, judgmental hate mongers with regards to homosexuals. The trend in American popular opinion is *that anyone who believes that homosexuality is sin* (i.e., Bible-believing Christians) *is evil,* and epitomizes what is wrong with our nation. With our president's declaration that "culture wars are so 90's," the impression is given that there is no place left for Christians to voice Biblical truth in the arena of public debate over such issues. And many in the Church are fearful to speak the truth that God loves sinners, but hates sin.

Sadly, there *are* some who attempt to hate groups of people in the name of Christ (and homosexuals are not their only target). However, even the casual observer of Scripture recognizes this is entirely against the message and example that Jesus gave us. He commanded us to love and bless even our enemies who hate and persecute us *(Matthew 5:44)*, and His life was wholly consistent with His teaching. Those who claim to use Scripture as a means of justifying hatred toward others are in serious deception, or are themselves deceivers. The more we become like our holy and merciful Savior, the more we will learn to simultaneously hate sin as He does *(Psalm 97:10; Romans 12:9; Jude 23)* and love sinners as He does *(Romans 5:8; Ephesians 2:4-5; John 3:16)*.

Attempting to practice one without the other always bears tragic fruit, and falls far short of the character of God in Christ.

Furthermore, an honest assessment of the Church today will quickly show that the average churchgoer does not fit the caricature drawn by the media. Millions of American Christians are decidedly *not* filled with hatred for homosexuals, and efforts to paint the Church as "homophobic" are simply propagandistic.

Ironically, a number of seeker-sensitive and "emergent church" leaders have bought the media's lie, and they are busying themselves with repenting to the homosexual community at large for how hateful we Christians are. Their message—especially influential among younger Believers—states that the Church has been a group of meanies for far too long, and the best thing we can do is just leave the whole issue of homosexuality alone. "Just let God do the judging," we are told, which really means, "just ignore what God's Word says, and instead follow an agenda of cultural acceptability and moral compromise." Such teaching is lauded by the world, by proponents of the homosexual agenda, and by Satan himself (where this teaching originates).

EMBRACING THEM TO DEATH

The politically correct "embracing" mindset toward homosexuality becoming pervasive within the Church (even among evangelicals) says in essence, *"Who are we to judge, everyone sins, their sin is no different than mine, let's just show love, only God decides who goes to hell anyway,"* etc. While this *appears* loving toward homosexuals and no doubt gives the adherents a warm and fuzzy feeling, it is—in the final analysis—every bit as unloving as the attitude of anger toward homosexuals. How so? Because while the mindset of embracing is probably well-intentioned and does make some true statements (such as "all have sinned," or "we should not judge"), it tries to excuse a lifestyle of persistent rebellion and breaking of God's moral law as being acceptable to Him, with the expectation that He will cut a "special deal" for such rebellion before His throne of judgment. The hypocrisy here is astounding! These Christians who warn against judging who goes to hell are quite willing to judge who goes to Heaven, as they (in essence) counsel the unrepentant homosexual that they will find special entry into God's heavenly Kingdom.

Christ died for sinners like you and me. Those who know how greatly they have been forgiven have no stones to throw at anyone; on the contrary, we who have been forgiven much must love much *(Luke 7:47)*. And the most loving thing God does for sinners is convict them of sin, for without conviction there will never be awareness of need, thus no forgiveness through Christ. The popular new "gospel" that avoids telling sinners about sin seems to have overlooked that **"the *GOODNESS* of God leads"** men and women **"to repentance"** *(Romans 2:4)*.

To encourage anyone to continue in a lifestyle of unrepentant sin (whether that sin is lying, violence, marital unfaithfulness, homosexuality, or any other) while giving them the impression that God is OK with their actions is (in reality) *to show no love whatsoever for that individual's life, whether in time or in eternity.*

The argument is often made that "all sin is the same; the Church only focuses on homosexuality because it's always easier to throw stones at someone else's sin than deal with our own." In fact, one well-known pastor/author/megachurch mogul has equated homosexuality with the sin of overeating (ironically, this man is quite overweight). Since God forgives sin, why should we worry about the homosexual's sin (especially when we are not particularly concerned about our own)? The logic seems sound at first, and many will take it as gospel truth simply because a substantial church figure has said it. But is it Biblical?

Though it sounds reasonable, such teaching confuses two separate issues: the *eternal impact* of sin, and the *temporal effects* of sin. *All* sin has the same impact as to our eternal destiny, for *any* sin is enough to make us worthy of judgment.

In that sense, all sin is the same, and lying or gluttony has the same impact as homosexuality or murder.

However, all sins do not have the same temporal effects on our lives. The more pervasive, controlling, and deeply ingrained a sin becomes, the more destructive its results will be in our lives. Sins that become a regular part of our lifestyle (such as alcoholism or pornography addiction, for instance) take the greatest toll on us, because they harden our heart, numb our conscience, ruin relationships, and destroy our hunger for fellowship with God. In short, *they destroy our lives*. And moreover, they greatly increase the odds that we will avoid a relationship with God altogether, and thus spend eternity paying the heavy price for our sin.

Homosexuality is a prime example of such a sin. It often becomes the very identity of the one caught therein, and exerts the primary influence over decisions regarding relationships, family, career, politics, and spirituality. Most sins exist in the realm of "something I do" (and soon regret); homosexuality lives in the realm of "who I am" and "why I live." For this reason, it is uniquely destructive in the life of the sinner.

God's heart is to seek and save the lost, but that requires that we admit we are lost. No one—not an adulterer or liar, not a thief or hater, not the proud nor the lustful—no one can excuse their sin and find forgiveness. To the angry man, the Spirit of God convicts him of his anger. Then he has a choice: repent of his anger (confess it as sinful, ask God to forgive him, and turn from his anger), or ignore the conviction of the Spirit and suffer eternally for having done so. The Holy Spirit will empower him to turn from his anger, but the man must make the decision to repent and thus open the door to the Spirit's power. Without genuine repentance, there will be no change.

Homosexuality is no exception—wholehearted repentance followed by crying out for the Spirit's help will result in a changed life, for God always keeps His word. *The path to freedom may be costly, and the battle may be great, but that is no excuse for staying in a life of sin.* Spurgeon wrote, "Better a brief warfare and eternal rest, than false peace and everlasting torment."

For the sake of perspective, let us look at a different (though related) area. Countless men in the Church today (*60–70%, according to recent surveys*) are caught in habitual heterosexual lust, and have been for many years. Breaking long-established strongholds of thought and behavior is daunting, and only possible by the application of God's Word under the power of God's Spirit. Many have attempted to effect change in their lives through hard-fought and sincere human effort, and have only met repeated defeat. This is the sad reality of the Church today (although it need not be so).

However, Christian leaders (seeing the difficulty these men are having) never offer them counsel such as, "It's OK—God made you this way. Others (especially your wife) need to learn to accept you as you are. Embrace your lust and live life to its fullest, knowing that God accepts you *just as you are!*" Such counsel would be ludicrous, but it is no less so when church leaders attempt to excuse homosexuality. Christ loves sinners (including homosexuals) enough to tell us the truth about our sin. Only then can the goodness of God lead us to repentance.

One further point should be made regarding the societal impact of homosexuality. In Romans chapter one, Paul shows what a society looks like when it is abandoning God, and widespread acceptance and promotion of homosexuality is a clear indicator that a nation is nearing the end of its moral rope. That those who claim to speak for Christ would be part of such promotion in our nation is beyond reprehensible. And that Christians are listening to such rubbish is indicative of how far we have fallen as a Church.

Before leaving this subject, we must lovingly confront a painful truth. For nearly 40 years, the Church has led the way in normalizing divorce in American culture. We have, from pulpit to pew, taken what God said He hates (*Malachi 2:13-17*) and called it acceptable. Under the guise of compassion we have attempted to lower the standard and authority of His Word in our lives and churches, thus trampling upon His grace. And the spiritual consequences (both in the Church and in our nation) have been nothing short of disastrous. In the pursuit of personal happiness we have made a mockery of God's holiness. And not surprisingly, the Church is neither happy nor holy as a result. If we are to return to a place of righteous influence in America, we must repent to God for how we have devalued the covenant of marriage. And we must begin to lead the way in the *right* direction by cultivating marriages that honor God... till death do us part.

RETURN TO AUTHORITY

For the American Church to return to her God-intended authority, we must lovingly and unapologetically speak the Truth of God's Word to our brothers and sisters in the Church. We must be uncompromising in our defense of the Truth, "in humility correcting those who are in opposition" as Paul wrote to Timothy *(2 Timothy 2:25)*. Remembering that the flesh profits nothing, we must be Spirit-led in how and when we engage the lost on issues of cultural impact, making certain that the fruit of our lives is always *love*. And most importantly, as we wage war in the secret place of prayer, we must believe and fully expect that God will once again shake our nation to its core, resulting in what could be the greatest spiritual awakening America has ever known.

Walking in true spiritual authority makes you a target, and the true Church will be opposed by the world and by hell. The cost to those who thus seek to honor the Lord will be high; however, the cost to our nation if we fail to obey will be inestimably higher. **We must return** to the place of our rightful authority. The path of return always begins with steps of *humility, prayer, seeking God's face,* and *repentance (2 Chronicles 7:14)*. If we in the Church return to these steps, **God will return to our land.**

CHAPTER 12

God's Promises for the Last Days' Church

WE ARE LIVING IN THE "PERILOUS TIMES" of which the Apostle Paul prophesied. Though these are days of great trial, they will prove to be days of unprecedented outpouring of the glory and power of the Most High. Those who love and seek the Lord will truly be "more than conquerors" through everything the world and our spiritual foes send against us. Weapons shall form against the people of God, but they shall not prosper, for He has promised to always lead us in triumph in Christ Jesus. If your heart is after Jesus, He will beautify and strengthen you through the battles you face, and make you a vessel of His love and glory.

God has always protected His children through the fires of adversity *(see Daniel 3)*, and He will do the same in the season ahead. As we draw deeply from the truth of God's Word, we find the promises of a perfectly loving and watchful Father to comfort, strengthen, and guide us through such a day. Scripture gives us God's instructions for His people living during "the end of the age" *(Matthew 24:3)*. If we take heed to His Word, it will be a rock beneath our feet and a light to our path during these trying times.

GOD CALLS HIS PEOPLE TO VICTORY THROUGH CONFLICT, BOTH PERSONAL AND CORPORATE

God desires a triumphant Church, but there can be no triumph without first having a fight. God will allow battles to touch our lives because He wants us to be "more than conquerors" through everything we face *(Romans 8:37)*, thus bringing Him great glory.

Paul wrote that "All who desire to live godly in Christ Jesus will suffer persecution" *(2 Timothy 3:12)*. For American Christians, this has come primarily in the form of spiritual warfare. Those who love and seek to glorify Christ have felt the "fiery darts" of the accuser come against relationships, health, families, finances, and ministry endeavors. While some popular Church personalities have preached that Christ's death and resurrection means we should experience a life free from battle or trouble, neither Scripture nor the history of the Church would agree.

Spurgeon wrote, "The best evidence of the Lord's presence is the devil's growl." If we are content to accomplish nothing for the Lord, Satan is content to let us. However, start pursuing the Lord and praying for revival, and one can be assured that the battle will engage.

TAKING IT TO THE STREETS

In the years ahead, we will see the spiritual battle become more external, fought in plain view of the public eye, especially in the courts and political arenas. Though the persecution may fall short of the imprisonment, torture, and martyrdom that our brothers and sisters experience in other parts of the world, opposition to Biblical Christianity will become more aggressive in America, and we will receive the blessing of paying a price for our faith. And this, beyond a shadow of doubt, will be the best thing that could happen to the American Church.

If open opposition sounds a bit ominous, God's Word offers us the best news imaginable: our victory is as sure as the Cross, as sure as the Resurrection, as sure as the ever-nearing Return of Christ. "In this world you will have tribulation," Jesus told His disciples. "But be of good cheer, **I have overcome the world**" *(John 16:33)*. And because His victory was absolutely final, ours is absolutely sure.

FROM FEARFUL, TO FEARLESS, TO FEARSOME

Numerically, the initial effect of persecution on the Church may look something like a "Gideon's revival," as the fair-weather sheep move on to greener grass on the other side of the cultural fence. But as those who remain in the fold draw nearer to their Savior, they will find themselves built up, prepared, and strengthened to be a mighty witness for Jesus Christ in our nation. Daniel wrote, "but the people who know their God shall be strong, and carry out great exploits" *(Daniel 11:32)*, and so shall it be with the Church.

God's plan is to "purify the sons of Levi" *(Malachi 3:3)*, that our worship and witness may be pure and powerful. We are God's "royal priesthood," ordained to bring Him praise and to be a witness to the world *(1 Peter 2:9)*. For those Christians whose hearts are set after their King, the opposition of man and economic uncertainty will only serve to deepen their faith, just as the roots of an oak tree grow deeper through the wind and storm. We will prove God to be "our refuge and strength, a very present help in trouble. **Therefore we will not fear**…" *(Psalm 46:1-2)*.

Not unlike the transformation that Peter experienced at Pentecost, Believers and churches will experience an increase in the power and presence of God in and through their lives and ministries. We will go deeper in our knowledge of God's

Word, become more prevailing in prayer, and our lives and fellowship will radiate the indwelling Presence of the Holy Spirit. While persecution may well prove to be the *catalyst* for such a transformation, the *power source* will be God alone. And our *motive* will be a personal love for Jesus and a passionate desire to see Him glorified in America once again. Many *will* count the cost, and innumerable souls will be saved in this last great spiritual harvest in our nation.

SHELTER THROUGH THE STORM

For many of us, the thought of persecution for Christ's sake is daunting. It can strike fear in our hearts as we consider, "What about my family's safety? What about our finances? Will our faith be sufficient to endure the storms that are coming?"

It is with great seriousness that we must embrace a specific word of peace and encouragement for God's people in the days ahead. While suffering for Christ is a Biblical promise, and we will no doubt experience persecution in the coming years, we must recognize that God's agenda for those who seek Him includes His presence for the days ahead.

> *The LORD is good,*
> *A stronghold in the day of trouble;*
> *And He knows those who trust in Him.*
>
> Nahum 1:7

While in the midst of proclaiming impending judgment on Israel, Isaiah was commanded by God to bring this word of comfort and protection to the righteous remnant:

> *Say to the righteous that it shall be well with them,*
> *For they shall eat the fruit of their doings.*
>
> Isaiah 3:10

Just as God protected and provided for His people in Goshen as the plagues were smiting Egypt, and just as He caused His wrath to pass over their homes when He saw the blood of the lamb on their doorposts, so God will watch over, protect, and provide for His own in the end times. But we must be careful to place our trust in Him alone, and not look to man and his systems as our defense or provider.

> *Blessed is the man who trusts in the LORD,*
> *and whose hope is the LORD.*
> *For he shall be like a tree planted by the waters,*
> *which spreads out its roots by the river,*
> *And will not fear when heat comes;*
> *But its leaf will be green,*
> *and will not be anxious in the year of drought,*
> *Nor will cease from yielding fruit.*
>
> Jeremiah 17:7-8

Self-preservation will prove fatal as we near Christ's return, for "he who seeks to save his life will lose it" *(Luke 17:33)*. Safety is found in being able to say with Paul, "I have been crucified with Christ; it is no longer I who live, but Christ lives in me, and the life which I now live in the flesh I live by faith in the Son of God, who loved me and gave Himself for me" *(Galatians 2:20)*. As we give ourselves *to* and *for* the One who gave Himself for us, we can rest assured that He will be faithful to guide and guard us. This is not to say that God promises to keep us from all trial and trouble, for such a promise does not exist in Scripture. Instead, we have a far better promise: *the Presence of God in the midst of our trials.*

> *When you pass through the waters,*
> *I will be with you;*
> *And through the rivers, they shall not overflow you.*

When you walk through the fire,
you shall not be burned,
Nor shall the flame scorch you.

Isaiah 43:1-2

Jesus promised to be with us "always, even to the end of the age" *(Matthew 28:20)*. And therein lies our peace, confidence, and trust. We will learn to dwell under the shadow of the Almighty once again *(Psalm 91:1)*.

RETURN TO THE OLD PATHS

Thus says the LORD: "Stand in the ways and see,
And ask for the old paths, where the good way is,
and walk in it;
Then you will find rest for your souls."

Jeremiah 6:16

God is calling His people back to the purity and simplicity of a living faith in Christ *(2 Corinthians 11:3)*, to a wholehearted devotion that will bear good fruit in our lives and churches. These "old paths" include:

RETURN TO OUR FIRST LOVE *(Revelation 2:4-5)*, where we make our love for Jesus the first priority in our lives. Spurgeon wrote, "*A jealous God will not be content with a divided heart; He must be loved first and best.*" **The most vital point of return is to a personal, passionate love for Christ**. All other efforts (regardless how zealous) will be fruitless without such love. We cannot start by championing the cause of family, or work ethic, or political activism, or even by crusading for our favorite doctrinal persuasion. The goal and fruit of our lives must be love, first for God and then for others *(Matthew 22:37-39)*, and that must be the focal point of our return.

Many today who are calling for a "reformation" of the Church are, with the best of intentions, placing much emphasis on informing the head (with one brand of systematic theology) while ignoring the heart. The result is often to prove Paul's words that "knowledge puffs up," while love *BUILDS* up the Believer and the Church *(1 Corinthians 8:1)*. Scripture calls us to make disciples of Jesus Christ, not of John Calvin or John Wesley (or any other man); to lead the lost to a Redeemer, not a reformer. Let us be careful whom we truly serve with our highest allegiance and fullest passion.

RETURN TO KINGDOM VALUES. This rekindled love for Christ will be borne out in how and where we invest our thoughts, affections, time, efforts, and finances. As we walk out God's priorities in these areas, it will prove effective at destroying the idolatry, self-centeredness, and pride that so often lurks undetected in our lives.

RETURN TO FAMILY. For decades the American Church has seen the family through the lens of the world. For many Christian men, personal career achievement and financial gain have taken priority over leading their families in the things of God. Many women have also bought the lie, as the plague of the "double-income family" mindset has settled in on the Church to the detriment of marriages and children. Too many families are running to stand still financially, paying interest debt on homes and possessions they cannot enjoy, and leaving their children's development and nurturing in the hands of daycare workers and state-run schools.

God is calling us to prioritize our families' spiritual health over material gain, for the one is eternal while the other will be consumed with fire. We must take whatever steps the Lord leads to nurture and prepare our families for the season to come. If we would "prepare the way of the Lord," we must lead the way in our marriages and families.

RETURN TO FELLOWSHIP. The days ahead will show us that we need one another, and God is calling us to return to genuine fellowship *now.* For many of us, this will mean placing Biblical priority on gathering with Believers, on being an active part of a local fellowship through serving and giving, and on using the gifts God has given us to build up His Church. "Lone Ranger" Christians will prove to be lone sheep, and they make quick prey for the wolves.

On this note, it is vital that we invest our lives in a local fellowship that is 1) seeking the Lord, 2) preaching God's entire Word with power, 3) walking in the Spirit, and 4) saving lost souls. Admittedly, there are many unhealthy fellowships and churches out there, and we have a responsibility to be careful under what fellowship and teaching we place our lives and families. It is a time for discerning the fruit of those with whom we would follow and serve in the Lord *(Matthew 7:15-23, Hebrews 13:7).*

RETURN TO BIBLICAL EXPECTANCY. God's people are supposed to live with a joyful, quickening anticipation of Jesus' return. Many Christians tell of having lived with such expectancy amid the tumultuous events of the early 1970's. Israel had just recaptured Jerusalem, America was in the midst of a terrible war, the energy crisis was in full swing, Communism was looming large, and the Jesus Movement had begun ushering thousands of young "hippies" into a relationship with Christ. The stage seemed set for history's final season, and many Christians believed that at any moment Jesus could split the eastern sky en route to the Mount of Olives.

The decadence and materialism of the 1980's and 1990's served to soften the Church and steal her expectation. As we now find ourselves entering into what may well be the most turbulent time our nation has ever known, it is vitally important that God's people recognize "the signs of the times" and live with a Biblical anticipation of Christ's soon return.

In recent decades the American Church has seen a plethora of Bible teachers expounding their personal views regarding the "end times," usually arriving at significantly different conclusions, but all equally convinced that theirs is the only correct position. The unhealthy result of this dogmatic approach has been to polarize the Church into two groups of people: one that focuses far too much on the Last Days and one that focuses far too little.

It is imperative that we study all of God's Word (including Daniel and Revelation), but that we do so with a teachable and humble heart. And it is just as crucial that we treat and engage our brothers and sisters in an attitude of love, grace, and meekness when we disagree (for we will at times, especially on this topic). Anyone who feels he has discovered all the end-time answers has not considered all the end-time questions. One day we will know in full; in the meantime, let us hold our convictions with humility. As we do, we just might learn something from one another. And moreover, we can show the world what *real* unity looks like, without compromising.

Getting on the Same Page

Without splitting eschatological hairs, God's people of various doctrinal backgrounds and persuasions can and must give a plain reading to Jesus' words regarding the period before His return, which He called "the end of the age." While we will not (and need not) agree on every detail of how and when Christ will return, Believers can embrace the major thrust of Jesus' teaching on the subject and let it form the basis of doctrinal unity.

I exhort you to read (and re-read) Matthew 24, Mark 13, and Luke 21, three accounts of Jesus' teaching regarding the season and events leading up to His return. In response to His disciples' question of *"What will be the sign of your return?"* Christ gave the following indicators:

1. **The advent of false messiahs and false prophets;
   many speaking falsely in Jesus' Name** (*Matthew 24:5;
   Mark 13:6; Luke 21:8*); **massive deception, so that all
   but a remnant will be deceived** (*Matthew 24:24; Mark
   13:22-23*).
2. **Increased wars and natural disasters** (*Matthew 24:6-7;
   Mark 13:7-8; Luke 21:9-11*).
3. **Persecution of God's people, hatred by the world,
   betrayal** (*Matthew 24:9-10; Mark 13:12-13; Luke
   21:16-17*).
4. **Lawlessness abounding, love growing cold**
   (*Matthew 24:12*).
5. **The Gospel of the Kingdom being preached "to all the
   world as a witness to all nations" (ethnicities), "and
   then the end will come"** (*Matthew 24:14; Mark 13:10*).
6. **Jerusalem surrounded and destroyed, then "trampled
   by Gentiles until the times of the Gentiles are fulfilled"**
   (*Luke 21:24*).

While the *precise* extent to which some of these signs have
been fulfilled may be difficult to pinpoint, an honest assessment of recent history can only lead to the conclusion that *we
are getting ever so near to Christ's return*. For instance:

- Consider the astronomical growth and worldwide reach
  of cults such as Mormonism and Jehovah's Witnesses,
  claiming to be the *true* church and speaking in Jesus'
  Name. Many false prophets have arisen in our culture,
  not to mention those within Christianity. And many
  now claim to be "Christ."
- As for wars and disasters, the 20th century saw an
  unprecedented increase in the *scope and severity* of
  warfare ("World Wars" involving every continent,
  ever-increasing technological advances, even nuclear

weaponry). And the 21st century has started out with an enormous volume of cataclysmic natural disasters all over the world (from massive earthquakes, to historic tsunamis, to record-breaking hurricanes).

- Christ predicted a rise in persecution before His return, and the 20th century saw more Christian martyrs than any other time in history; in fact, it is estimated that of all the martyrs since Pentecost, *over 65% of them were killed during the last 100 years.*

- As for "lawlessness" abounding, even the secular pundits recognize that our society is plummeting in a moral free fall without a parachute, although they diagnose only symptoms (for the root cause is spiritual). Jesus' prediction of lawlessness is coming to pass in our day, reflected in the massive increase of deadly violence in schools, in the unprecedented attack on the institution of marriage, in the increased number of addicts on our streets, in the overcrowded conditions in our nation's prisons, and in 50 million babies aborted in the last several decades.

And yet, these trends are but the logical fruit of America abandoning her belief in God, Scripture, and morals. Any nation that sows godlessness will reap lawlessness. *We can expect the world to behave like the world.* However, the most ominous and unfathomable trend in our nation is the *widespread lawlessness on the part of those who claim the name of Christ.* Amid all the turmoil of our day, the Church has been largely self-consumed, ignorant of the temporal needs and apathetic concerning the eternal destinies of the lost. Love is growing cold, even within the Church.

- Jesus stated plainly that the "Gospel of the Kingdom" would be preached "to all nations" in the days before His return. Missiologists (those who collect and study data regarding worldwide missions) report that we are growing significantly closer to achieving this goal, and some anticipate its accomplishment within approximately 20 years.

- Lastly, Jesus made two specific points regarding Jerusalem: it would be destroyed, and then "trampled by Gentiles" until a specific point in the future ("until the times of the Gentiles are fulfilled"). Both of His statements have come to pass.

In 70 A.D., Roman troops (led by Titus) destroyed the Temple and devastated the city. For the next 1900 years, Gentile nations (including the Turks, Arabs, and even the British) had political and military control over Jerusalem. During this period, the fulfillment of the rest of Jesus' prophesy regarding Jerusalem was viewed by many in Christendom as being purely symbolic, since Israel was quite literally "blown off the map," having ceased from being a national entity for 19 centuries. Then on May 14th, 1948, God—who sits enthroned above the heavens and oversees the boundaries of the nations *(Acts 17:26)*—caused Israel to arise from the ashes of the Holocaust. In one day Israel was reborn, in fulfillment of Isaiah 66:8.

In 1967 Israel fought a coalition of Arab nations in what would be called the "Six Day War." Although massively outnumbered and surrounded by foes on three sides (and the Mediterranean Sea on the other), Israel experienced amazing victories, defeating the coalition's armies in less than one week's time. And in the process, Israel recaptured Jerusalem, thus fulfilling that portion of Jesus' prophecy regarding the place He called, "the city of the great King" *(Matthew 5:35)*. Jerusalem was under Jewish rule for the first time in roughly two millennia, and the period Jesus called "the times of the Gentiles" must logically be seen as being "fulfilled" *(Luke 21:24)*.

Jesus' statement in Luke 21 indicates that the priority of prophetic events has swung back to the descendants of Abraham, whereas for the past 2,000 years the priority largely centered on taking the Good News to the Gentile people groups spread over the earth. Jesus' words coincide with Paul's words in Romans 11:23-27 that spiritual renewal would occur on a large scale among the Jewish people once "the fullness of the Gentiles has come in" to faith in Christ. Not surprisingly, Jewish evangelism experts point to an unprecedented rise in Jewish people coming to faith in Jesus beginning in the year 1967, the same year that Israel recaptured Jerusalem. In fact, 1967 is generally regarded as the birth of the modern "Messianic Jewish movement." Both the nearness of world evangelism being completed and the events of 1967 should give us great anticipation for the season in which God has placed us.

THE ULTIMATE RETURN

The significant extent to which Jesus' first six points have been (and are being) fulfilled gives us clear indication that we are drawing nearer to the last two points of Jesus' prophecy:

1. **The greatest tribulation ever known to man; and**
2. **Christ's triumphant return.**

Jesus told us not to speculate as to the specific day and hour of His return, although many have ignored that command to their own shame (remember the book *88 Reasons Why Jesus is Coming Back in 1988*?) God holds the times and seasons in His own hand, and He does not solicit our opinion as to how and when they should take place (and whether or not it happens as our favorite end-time novel series depicted it).

However, in the light of Scripture and of the events of our day, **it is entirely responsible to say that we are likely living in the final generation before His return;** in fact, to say otherwise is to ignore the "signs of the times" for which Jesus told us to look.

As such, the final two points of Jesus' prophecy are breath-takingly close, and the response of our hearts should be that of joyous, overcoming, expectant faith. However, the part of us that is attached to the things of this world will not rejoice at such news. My wife was recently teaching our eight year-old son about longing for Jesus' return. He replied with fervency, "Yes, I **really** want Jesus to come back soon... but not before Christmas."

We adults can identify with those feelings, although we are seldom so honest about it. To the extent that we have invested our hearts in the wrong treasure, we will experience angst rather than anticipation at the thought of experiencing the end of the age, for Christ said, "Where your treasure is, there your heart will be also" *(Matthew 6:21)*. The world is driven by self-preservation, while the place of true peace and safety is in already having been "crucified with Christ" *(Galatians 2:20)*, and in knowing that our loving Father will use us for His greatest glory, both in life and in death.

We need have no fear of the future, but rather a great expectation of our Savior's soon return. The greatest outpouring of God's power and glory are so close at hand. Let us make our lives, our families, and our churches ready for His return.

> *Therefore, since all these things will be dissolved,*
> *what manner of persons ought you to be*
> *in holy conduct and godliness,*
> *looking for and hastening*
> *the coming of the day of God...*
>
> 2 Peter 3:11-12

CHAPTER 13

A Word to the Weary

FOR TOO MANY CHRISTIANS in our generation, the American Church has not been a welcoming place, and serving therein has been no picnic. If we are honest, those of us who have served in roles of church leadership will readily acknowledge that we have all fallen short, and have at times caused hurt to the very ones we were trying to serve. The common model of "top down" leadership, where elders operate as a corporate committee and the senior pastor as a CEO, has been a natural breeding ground for the "lording it over" style of leadership that Jesus commanded us to avoid. This closing chapter is not intended to be an indictment of church leadership, but a word of hope, blessing, and encouragement to those who have experienced pain and rejection due to circumstances and individuals in the American Church.

REJECTED BY MAN, ACCEPTED BY GOD

When a young follower of Jesus accepts the call to "take up your cross and follow Me," he or she never imagines that part of his or her crucifixion could come at the hands of the institutional Church. After all, we are all part of the same Body, called to carry forth the same Good News, and to share the same fellowship in Christ.

And yet it is a tragically common theme: sincere Believers in Jesus enter into the local church, devoted and dedicated, eager to serve the Lord and His people. What they receive at the hands of church leadership may bear little resemblance to what Scripture teaches, and the hurts experienced can be deep and impacting. After lengthy effort these Christians exit the church as the "walking wounded," jaded toward the Body of Christ and suffering in their faith. Some experience wounds that linger for years to come; and meanwhile, life goes on "business as usual" in the church where the hurt has occurred.

For those who have suffered under abusive religious leadership, please hear these words of encouragement from the heart of a shepherd who loves God's people, and who has been through a few fires himself. My friend, it is vital to remember that you are walking a path first trod by our Savior. Jesus' greatest resistance came from religious leadership, those who possessed positions of authority but had lost God's heart for His people (or perhaps never had it to begin with). Pharisees still exist in the American Church today, and if you have been rejected by such, please do not accept the report of shame and worthlessness that often follows. Remember: the rejection of man often indicates the acceptance and pleasure of God.

To those who have been betrayed by other Christians, remember that you are following in the footsteps of your Master who was betrayed for you. Count it joy, then, to suffer in like manner for Him. Pull the knife out of your back, choose to forgive those who you feel have so deeply wronged you, and choose to follow Christ again with all your heart, for He is worthy of no less. *"Great hearts can only be made by great troubles,"* wrote Spurgeon. Betrayal is such a "great trouble," and God can use it for good in the end, making you a vessel of healing and comfort in the lives of others who have been similarly hurt. As you allow God's grace to operate through your life in this area, you take what Satan meant for evil and allow God to be glorified through it.

For those whose faith has been battered by the downfall of a Christian leader whom you greatly respected, please receive this difficult but urgent exhortation: *choose to forgive them.* Make no excuses for their sin, learn from their mistakes, gain a deeper fear of the Lord through the experience; but throw no stones. It is a tragic reality that sometimes Christian leaders stray from their First Love, allowing their personal devotion to Christ to take the backseat to other endeavors and priorities... and that is when the danger begins. At such times men do fail and fall, for Satan knows well the principle: "strike the shepherd, and the sheep will be scattered" *(Zechariah 13:7).* We must be those whose faith is so deeply anchored in the unfailing love of a faultless Savior that the imperfections and sinful actions of man cannot shake us. Then we can be used by God to help rescue some of the "scattered sheep" who are still hurting from the sins of a fallen leader.

Lastly, here is a daring word of exhortation to those disenfranchised from the Church: *get back in the battle.* You may have been wronged, betrayed, and kicked to the curb at the hands of organized religion. The great British preacher Dr. Martyn Lloyd Jones once said, "Religion has often been the greatest and the most bitter enemy of spiritual truth." You may have personally (painfully) experienced the reality of his statement.

However, you are called to be a disciple of Christ, to carry your cross, to suffer for the Savior, and to serve the King. *Jesus never gave up, and neither can you.* Ask God for a way to re-engage the battle, to "re-enlist" in His army, and then take your post. This may start simply by praying for our nation and the Church every day, but it will certainly lead you back into relationships where you serve His Body again.

"Dear God, how?" some will say. "After all I have been through, how can I ever trust or serve in the Church again?"

The pain in such a question is palpable (in fact, the author has felt it firsthand). However, the return of the disenfranchised Christians to Jesus' Church is a vital element of the return of the American Church as a whole. Many who have been scattered may be gifted and anointed ministers, possessing devotion and discernment that are irreplaceable. We desperately need you to be an active part of the Body of Christ.

What that will look like will vary from one Christian to the next. There are many expressions of the Church in our culture today, from the "typical" Sunday morning variety, to house churches, to family-integrated churches, and others. The vital point is not the external form but the internal spiritual health. You are not hereby encouraged to re-enter an unhealthy church environment, nor to offer yourself up as a "sheep among wolves" once again. Be wise and discerning in the way you seek out a church fellowship, and above all be prayerful and humble.

Ask God to guide you to a fellowship that is *healthy* (not perfect). The more discernment you possess, the more swiftly you will find problems and imperfections with any and all church fellowships you visit. While there are no perfect churches, there are yet *healthy* fellowships where God's Word is spoken in love and power *(Ephesians 4:15)*, where Believers are knit together in loving relationships *(Acts 2:46)*, where God is worshiped in Spirit and truth *(John 4:23-24)*, and where the Christian learns to be a disciple, growing in the likeness of Christ *(Romans 12:2)*.

Finding problems in the American Church today is like shooting fish in a barrel; working toward God's solution is a much larger task, one worthy of our service and love. Remember, our serving in the Body is for Jesus first and foremost. *You and I can risk being hurt again, if it means bringing glory to our King.*

And in reality, we *will* experience hurt again, in some relationship or aspect of church involvement. We must be quick to forgive, quick to get God's heart for those who have wronged us, and quick to move on. Does this sound difficult? It is not difficult—it is impossible, humanly speaking. That is why we need (and can fully expect) the help and grace of the Holy Spirit. *He will heal our hearts as we re-engage the arena in which we were hurt.* As long as you keep yourself from all fellowship, you will never be *fully* healed from the wounds you experienced from fellowships past.

The American Church has dire need for the return of her disenfranchised members. For the glory of the King and the good of His people, I adjure you to prayerfully return to your calling. If you seek Him for the particulars, He will guide you in His path of return, give you all the grace you need, and heal your heart in the process. I know, for I have walked this path myself.

Now...

To Him who is able to
keep you from stumbling,
And to present you faultless
before the presence
of His glory with exceeding joy...

To Him who is able to do exceedingly
abundantly above all that we ask or think,
according to the power that works in us,
to Him be glory in the church
by Christ Jesus to all generations,
forever and ever. Amen.

Heart-Probing Questions on the Road of Return

CHAPTER 1 ~ THE TIME OF SHAKING HAS BEGUN

1. Do you believe we are experiencing the prophesied Last Days shaking?

2. A Christian's response to "shaking" should differ drastically from the unbeliever's response. In what ways has this shaking affected your own life? In what ways have you given in to fear? And what steps will you take to consistently walk in "perfect love" which "casts out fear" *(1 John 4:18)*?

3. The author states that *"the world desperately needs to see a people decidedly NOT like themselves, a people set apart to serve a different God, pursue a different kingdom, and follow a different definition of success."* What is your definition of success? In what ways have you succumbed to worldly thinking? In what ways are you actively seeking God, and making His glory the highest goal of your life?

4. **Read Luke 12:15-34**, wherein Jesus contrasts two kingdoms, two mindsets, and two ways of handling wealth. Prayerfully consider: *"Are there unnecessary possessions in my life that are hindering my friendship with Christ? Have I allowed finances (or the pursuit thereof) to become a distraction from loving and serving God? Do I own things, or do my things own me?"*

5. **Ministry leaders:** Shaking in our nation presents great opportunity for the Church. How can you lead those in your sphere

of influence (whether fellow ministers, friends, or those in your family and church) in prayer for our nation? What changes should the "shaking" bring about in your own life? How would the Lord have you prepare those under your ministry to be ready for even further shaking in our nation?

CHAPTER 2 ~ MISSING: THE PRESENCE OF GOD

1. The New Testament shows the normative Christian life as being lived under the guidance and power of the Holy Spirit *(see Romans 8:13-14)*. Do you ask for His leading and empowering in your daily life? If not, will you begin?

2. What attitudes, behaviors, or practices are frustrating the fullness of God's presence in your life?

3. Since we are temples of the Holy Spirit *(see 1 Corinthians 6:19)*, how can you make more room for the Spirit's presence in the temple of your life? *What things need to be discarded to facilitate His power and presence working through you?*

4. **Ministry leaders:** In what areas or ways have you attempted to do *"God's work man's way,"* relying on your own gifts and abilities rather than on the wisdom and power of God? What parts of your present ministry need to be "resubmitted" to the Lordship and leading of Jesus? What does the pattern of "Wait... Receive... *then* Advance" look like in your life and ministry?

CHAPTER 3 ~ AMERICAN WORSHIP: TWIN TRAGEDIES

1. Consider your favorite Christian leader, speaker, author, or singer. *What is the difference between appreciating their ministry and idolizing them?* Do you see in your life or congregation the subtle substitution of worship of man for true worship of God? In what ways?

2. Ultimately, our public worship of God will go no deeper than our private communion with Him. With this in mind, are you cultivating a personal, passionate devotion for Christ? Where do you fall short? How are you making worship a regular part of your life, outside of corporate settings?

3. The majority of American Christians claim they have never experienced God's presence in a worship service. How will you be a part of reversing this trend? In what ways will you welcome and prioritize God's presence amongst God's people in corporate worship? How can you encourage those in your sphere of influence to develop a growing personal experience of God's presence in their daily lives? How might this begin in your family?

4. **Ministry leaders:** In light of the quote in this chapter from Robert Murray McCheyne, what does it mean to "preach Christ for Christ's sake?" *Identify ways in which your ministry tends to attract people to yourself, contrasted by those ways in which your ministry attracts them to Christ.*

CHAPTER 4 ~ AMERICA: THE COMPROMISED CHURCH

1. Being mindful of the tragic consequences Israel experienced due to her compromise of God's commands *(see Numbers 25)*, identify the main areas of compromise in your own life. Are you willing to 1) surrender afresh those areas to the Lord, 2) ask for the Spirit's guidance and power to help you, and 3) take tangible steps (such as confession, repentance, and accountability) to honor God in those areas of weakness?

2. Contrast the author's description of "holiness" and being "sanctified" with the common misconceptions in the Church today. Have you experienced confusion over what it really means to be "sanctified?" Do you have negative ideas regarding holiness that you need to replace with what God's Word really says?

3. **Ministry leaders:** Eleven indispensable "Biblical pillars" have been commonly compromised, in whole or in part, within the modern American Church. Identify: *Which of these pillars are present in your own ministry? Which ones are missing? Which have been compromised... how... and why?*

CHAPTER 5 ~ NEW CROSS, NO CROSS

1. Re-read the eight elements of *"The Original Gospel"* shared in this chapter. Have you embraced each of those aspects of the

Gospel in your own life? What parts are missing? Are you willing to ask God to fulfill His Word in and through your life in all of these areas?

2. In the light of the section entitled *"Real Righteousness by Simple Faith,"* have you received God's gift of righteousness by faith (just as you received salvation)? In what ways are you striving to "save yourself" by self-effort? As you identify those areas, *surrender them to the Lord,* repenting of all self-reliance, and invite His Spirit to be your strength *(Ephesians 3:16)*. Will you allow yourself to be truly led by both the Word and Spirit of God into a **walk** of righteousness that brings true peace?

3. Scripture promises the Believer a life of consistent victory over sin by the power of the Holy Spirit *(Romans 8:13)*. In what ways are you relying upon and experiencing this power in your daily life? In what ways are you experiencing defeat? Overcoming sin absolutely requires dependence on the Spirit's power, but we must submit our will and ways to His. Are you constantly trying to "resist the devil," or are you first "submitting to God" (James 4:7)?

4. What does it mean to "take up your cross" in your personal life? How do you express self-denial and sacrifice? How are you leading your family or friends, making disciples who prioritize God's glory over the pursuit of personal happiness?

5. **Ministry leaders:** What elements of *"The Original Gospel"* are present and prevalent in your own ministry? In which of those elements are you weakest? Why? Will you ask God to transform those areas of weakness, and to guide you in boldly holding forth the full Biblical Gospel?

CHAPTER 6 ~ PURPOSE OR PASSION?

1. What would you describe as the driving force or primary pursuit of your life? How does that determine your decision-making, goal-setting, and priorities?

2. *"A passion for God's glory will prove to be a source of strength and clarity amid turbulent times."* Do you possess a conscious

passion for God to be glorified through your life? Do you believe your faith is prepared to thrive in a season of severe shaking? What steps can you take to cultivate this in your life?

3. **Ministry leaders:** With so many programs and fads sweeping through the Church, how do you determine what is a worthy tool to share with those whom God has called you to lead? What means do you use to test the fruit of a program or study tool? How are you cultivating a deeper personal passion for God's glory through your own life, and in your family?

CHAPTER 7 ~ CHEAP GRACE, EASY BELIEVISM, AND SELF-LOVE

1. Using Hebrews 4:16 as a starting point, what are some of the Biblical distinctives between "mercy" and "grace?" How are these displayed in your life?

2. Why do you think the American Church has bought in so deeply to the idea of "grace" being merely an excuse for sin?

3. Consider the Scriptural correlation described in this chapter between *loving* Jesus and *obeying* Him. Does this differ from what you have been taught in church environments?

4. The author describes obedience as *"a loving response to the Savior, not a legalistic effort to earn His favor."* Since Jesus' goal is the right thing (obedience) for the right reason (love), what are some *other* (unworthy) motivations that are commonly used to attempt to effect obedience in Christian's lives?

5. **Ministry leaders: Re-read** the final three paragraphs of this chapter, and ask yourself: "What concrete steps am I going to take to rekindle the flame of my First Love, to prioritize personal communion with Christ, to seek Him for revival in those He has called me to lead, and to become the message without hypocrisy?" *Write these steps down,* share them with a close friend or ministry partner, and set measurable goals in your pursuit. Then ask your friend or ministry partner to *hold you accountable,* checking weekly to see how well you are tending the altar of your heart after Jesus.

CHAPTER 8 ~ WARNING:
AN EMERGENT-C IN THE CHURCH

1. "Relevance" is a catchphrase often heard in the Church today. But what makes someone or something *truly* relevant to the lost... or even to Believers?

2. *Discerning the Fruit:* using Hudson Taylor and David Wilkerson as examples, what fruits should God's people look for in the lives and ministries of those whom we choose to follow?

3. Paul wrote that "All things are lawful for me, but not all things are profitable." What are some "permissible" things that you have chosen to forego for the sake of loving God and others?

4. Consider Dietrich Bonhoeffer's words: "When Christ calls a man, He bids him come and die." What does this look like in your life?

5. The author writes, "The life you seek will never be found by seeking life, but only by seeking to bring glory to Christ. *As you live for the King of Glory, your life will reflect the glory of the King.*" Are you letting any motivation—whether fear, self-love, pride, or otherwise—steal your joy in living your life for Christ's glory alone? Are there any steps of love, faith, and obedience that you feel led to take?

6. **Ministry leaders:** As the mindsets of the world exemplified by the Emergent movement are becoming increasingly prevalent within the Church as a whole, what steps are you taking to actively lead those in your ministry in the mindset of Christ?

CHAPTER 9 ~ OF SHEPHERDS AND KINGS

1. Most Christians with much church experience have likely seen both the "Rehoboam" style and servant-hearted leadership exemplified. Contrast the long-term fruits you have seen in fellowships under both styles of leadership.

2. Considering that a "pastor" is literally to be a "shepherd" of God's flock, what character and leadership traits should be evident in the life of one called to pastor?

3. What Christian authors have proved to be a blessing in your walk with Christ? How many books have you read by any of the "elders" listed in this chapter? *This week, invest in your friendship with Jesus: purchase a classic devotional work, and a biography of a great saint who has gone before us.*

4. **Ministry leaders:** Upon reading the seven points listed at the end of this chapter, any honest minister will see that he or she has fallen short in some way (or ways). **Identify** which points apply to you, **repent** for any related sin, and **take steps** of returning to God's plan for leaders.

CHAPTER 10 ~ GOD'S PLAN FOR A GLORIOUS CHURCH

1. "Self-discovery" is an increasingly common theme in popular Christianity of late. Biblically speaking, what is wrong with such a concept? How exactly does it fly in the face of the message and life of our Savior?

2. In this chapter (as well as others), the author presents the challenge to "press in" to the Lord, to pursue His presence and seek Him for revival. What does it mean to *seek* the Lord? What has that looked like in your own life? Using Hebrews 11:6 as a basis, contrast an *active* faith that seeks and pleases God with the *passive* concept of faith so prevalent in the Church today.

3. **Ministry leaders:** The statement, *"living for the glory of God, the good of His Church, and for the saving of lost souls"* sounds today like a description of a superlative Believer or spiritual giant, when in fact it ought to describe the average Biblical Christian. What has occurred to so weaken the American Church that the normative Believer is nominal, and the true disciple who seeks God is regarded as an anomaly? How would others describe *your* life? *What steps can you take to inspire and equip those entrusted to your spiritual care to become true disciples who love the Lord, know His Word, and walk in the power of the Spirit?*

CHAPTER 11 ~ SATAN'S AGENDA FOR OUR NATION

1. The author states that although the American Church is in a desperate place, *"There is no end to what God can do through even*

one who will believe and pray." What does that look like in your own life? And how can you lovingly challenge other Believers with an awareness of the Church's dire need and the imperativeness of prayer?

2. Remembering that "to obey is better than sacrifice" (I Samuel 15:22), do you believe that prayer is ever a substitute for obedience to God? How must prayer and intercession translate into action?

3. Why is the widespread acceptance of homosexuality gaining ground in the Church, in spite of the clarity of Scripture on the matter? Why are some evangelical leaders apt to create a special category of permissiveness for this sin that they would not create for heterosexual lust or other sins?

4. How has divorce and remarriage become normative in the Church in just one generation? What part have you played in this travesty?

5. **Ministry leaders:** Have you ever been tempted to compromise the truth of God's Word in an area of potential controversy due to cultural pressure or "political correctness?" Practically speaking, what does it look like to "hold fast the word of life" in an age of gross spiritual darkness *(Philippians 2:15-16)*? And how can you equip those in your ministry to do the same?

CHAPTER 12 ~ GOD'S PROMISES FOR THE LAST DAYS' CHURCH

1. The author writes, "If your heart is after Jesus, He will beautify and strengthen you through the battles you face, and make you a vessel of His love and glory." How have you seen God's goodness through the battles in your past? In what ways have you seen God receive glory and impart blessing through trials? And how can those mercies past inform and inspire our hearts to trust God for mercies present and future?

2. With popular culture viewing true Christianity as increasingly *un*popular, what does the phrase, "From Fearful... to Fearless... to Fearsome" mean to the Church? What does it mean in your own life?

3. In the light of the suffering being experienced by our brothers and sisters in nations like North Korea, China, and many others, how can we prepare for the days ahead and the suffering that may be coming to our own nation? Discuss the dangers of self-preservation as contrasted with the place of safety and peace described in Galatians 2:20.

4. This chapter lists five primary areas of "Return." Which one(s) speak most directly to your heart, and what concrete steps will you take to respond to the Lord's conviction and encouragement?

5. **Ministry leaders:** How can you impart in those you lead a sense of Biblical expectancy regarding Christ's return? How can you help your church or fellowship develop a healthy, balanced understanding of eschatology that bears the fruit of greater love for Christ and deeper burden for souls? And using Hebrews 13:3 as the model, how can you (practically speaking) mobilize those in your ministry to fervent prayer for our brethren in the Suffering Church?

CHAPTER 13 ~ A WORD TO THE WEARY

1. Have you ever been faced with rejection for trying to serve Jesus? If so, what did you learn from the experience, and what did God impart *to* you that He can minister *through* you to others who experience similar pain?

2. Consider the greatest grief you have known at the hands of organized religion. Have you forgiven those who caused the hurt? Have you prayed God's blessing over their life? Have you gained God's heart of mercy and compassion toward those who hurt you, even if their own heart is yet unrepentant?

3. If you find yourself among the many "disenfranchised" from the Church, what are your thoughts about the author's challenge to "re-engage the battle?" What step is the Lord leading you to take toward re-establishing fellowship with God's people? How does a willingness to suffer wrong for Christ's sake help guard your heart against the fear of being hurt again?

4. **Ministry leaders:** In the light of the tragically common abuses of power by leaders in the Church, how can we model a servant-hearted, sacrificial style of leadership? What steps can you take to make your ministry a place of safety and healing for those who have been wounded at the hands of religious leadership, while yet preserving Biblical church discipline and proclaiming God's Word without compromise?

Thus says the LORD…
"Return to Me, and I will return to you."

TO CONTACT THE PUBLISHER

Elijah Books
P.O. Box 70879
Richmond VA 23255
(804) 754-3000

elijahbooks@comcast.net
www.elijahbooks.com

TO CONTACT THE AUTHOR

Matthew Casey
P.O. Box 301368
Portland OR 97294

matthew@family.net
www.matthewcasey.org